KT-556-36.

# The College of Law
of England and Wales

Available soon:

For more information visit our web site
www.oup.co.uk/general/vsi/

Raymond Wacks

# PRIVACY

A Very Short Introduction

OXFORD
UNIVERSITY PRESS

# OXFORD
## UNIVERSITY PRESS

Great Clarendon Street, Oxford OX2 6DP

Oxford University Press is a department of the University of Oxford.
It furthers the University's objective of excellence in research, scholarship,
and education by publishing worldwide in

Oxford New York

Auckland Cape Town Dar es Salaam Hong Kong Karachi
Kuala Lumpur Madrid Melbourne Mexico City Nairobi
New Delhi Shanghai Taipei Toronto

With offices in

Argentina Austria Brazil Chile Czech Republic France Greece
Guatemala Hungary Italy Japan Poland Portugal Singapore
South Korea Switzerland Thailand Turkey Ukraine Vietnam

Oxford is a registered trade mark of Oxford University Press
in the UK and in certain other countries

Published in the United States
by Oxford University Press Inc., New York

British Library Cataloguing in Publication Data

Data available

Library of Congress Cataloging in Publication Data

Data available

Typeset by SPI Publisher Services, Pondicherry, India
Printed in Great Britain by
Ashford Colour Press Ltd, Gosport, Hampshire

ISBN 978-0-19-955653-3

1 3 5 7 9 10 8 6 4 2

# Contents

# Preface

Scarcely a day passes without reports of yet another onslaught on our privacy. Almost exactly thirty years ago I published another small book on this contentious subject. Reading *The Protection of Privacy* now, one is inescapably struck by the tectonic shifts wrought by advances in technology. Most conspicuous, of course, is the fragility of personal information online. Other threats generated by the digital world abound: innovations in biometrics, CCTV surveillance, Radio Frequency Identification (RFID) systems, smart identity cards, and the manifold anti-terrorist measures all pose threats to this fundamental value – even in democratic societies. At the same time, however, the disconcerting explosion of private data through the growth of blogs, social networking sites, such as MySpace, Facebook, YouTube, Twitter, and other contrivances of the Information Age render simple generalities about the significance of privacy problematic. The advent of Web 2.0 has enlarged the Internet from an information provider to a community creator. And the insatiable hunger for gossip continues to fuel sensationalist media that frequently degrade the notion of a private domain to which we legitimately lay claim. Celebrity is indefensibly deemed a licence to intrude.

The manner in which information is collected, stored, exchanged, and used has changed forever – and with it, the character of the threats to individual privacy. But while the electronic revolution touches almost every part of our lives, it is not, of course, technology itself that is the villain, but the uses to which it is put. Only this week I learned of a proposal in the Philippines to employ RFID chips, widely used for tracking goods and patients' medical data, to protect school pupils against kidnapping. Inserting a chip below the skin (like my dog has) would plainly have several positive advantages in tracing missing individuals, including those afflicted with dementia. But is the price too high? Do we remain a free society when we surrender our right to be unobserved – even when the ends are beneficial?

Notwithstanding these extraordinary technical developments, many of the problems I considered in 1980 have not fundamentally altered. Indeed, it is mildly reassuring to discover that I can find little to disagree with in my analysis of the central questions of privacy in that book and other writings over the last three decades! I could, of course, be wrong. But, despite the passage of more than thirty years, I still think that the generous extension of privacy to 'decisional' matters (abortion, contraception, sexual preference), and the (understandable) conflation with freedom and autonomy that it engenders, is a mistake. And I draw some comfort from the fact that in the ever-increasing dystopian prognoses of privacy's decline, rarely is mention made of these and other 'decisional' matters that often infiltrate into the province of privacy. Privacy advocates seldom agonize about these questions, important though they are, when they warn of the countless dangers posed by our information society. Is this a tacit acknowledgment that the true meaning of privacy corresponds with our intuitive understanding and use of the concept? Is privacy not primarily an interest in protecting sensitive information? When we lament its demise, do we not mourn the loss of control over intimate facts about ourselves? And the essence of that control is the explicit exercise of autonomy in respect of our most intimate particulars, whether they be pried upon or gratuitously published.

But perhaps this approach is misguided? Why should disparate privacy rights be unable to co-exist as different, but related, dimensions of the same fundamental idea? Why not allow 'informational privacy' to live in peace with 'decisional privacy'? Ironically, I think the lop-sided neglect of the former, and constitutional acceleration of the latter by the United States Supreme Court may now have come full circle, and that there are small signs of a belated recognition of the urgent need legally to protect personal information along European lines, as described in the pages that follow. It is important to clarify that my resistance to the equation of privacy and autonomy springs not from a denial of the importance of rights or even their formulation in broad terms which facilitate their legal recognition. It rests instead on the belief that by addressing the problem as the protection of personal information, the pervasive difficulties that are generally forced into the straitjacket of privacy might more readily be resolved. The concept of privacy has become too vague and unwieldy a concept to perform useful analytical work. This ambiguity has actually undermined the importance of this value and encumbered its effective protection.

My association with privacy and data protection has largely been from a legal perspective. But, although the law is an indispensable instrument in the protection of privacy, the subject obviously teems with a number of other dimensions – social, cultural, political, psychological, and philosophical, and I attempt here to consider these – and several other – forces that shape our understanding of this challenging concept.

My privacy journey began many moons ago as a research student in Oxford. Both the literature (predominantly American) and the legislation (principally Scandinavian) were thin on the ground. The first generation of data protection laws were still embryonic. Since those innocent days the position has, of course, changed beyond recognition. To describe this phenomenon as an explosion is no hyperbole. My foray into the field originated as an academic endeavour to elucidate the elusive notion of privacy. But the practical dimensions of this increasingly vulnerable right were never far away. Nor could they be; the Information Age was looming. The binary universe and its manifold digital incarnations along with new, sophisticated electronic surveillance devices and an audaciously invasive press rendered any complacency about the security of personal information ingenuous. I have, moreover, been fortunate to serve on a number of law reform and other committees dedicated to illuminating the protean nature of privacy, and formulating measures by which it might be protected. The experience gained from these opportunities has exerted a powerful influence on my understanding of and judgment about privacy and data protection. I am grateful to members of the Law Reform Commission of Hong Kong privacy sub-committee from whom I have learned so much.

The campaign to defend and preserve our privacy is indefatigably waged by several public interest research and advocacy groups around the world. This precarious frontline is patrolled by various remarkable individuals to whom a considerable debt is owed. Not only do these organizations, notably the Electronic Privacy Information Center (EPIC) in the United States, and Privacy International in Britain, champion the cause of privacy, but they undertake scrupulous research into, and provide regular intelligence on, almost every conceivable aspect of the subject, including the – often parlous – state of privacy in many jurisdictions. I salute, in particular, David Banisar, Roger Clarke, Simon Davies, Gus Hosein, and Marc Rotenberg. Among the numerous fruits of the labour of these and other individuals and groups is an important recent declaration on the future of privacy signed in Madrid in November 2009 by more than a hundred non-governmental organizations and privacy experts from over 40 countries. Though it was finalized only after this book was in press, it has been possible to include the text as an annex.

A distinguished group of colleagues, privacy commissioners, and other boffins have, over the years, provided encouragement, advice, and assistance in countless ways. Thanks are due to John Bacon-Shone, Eric Barendt, Colin Bennett, Mark Berthold, Jon Bing, the late Peter Birks, Michael Bryan, Ann Cavoukian, David Flaherty, Graham Greenleaf, Godfrey Kan, Michael Kirby, Stephen Lau, Charles Raab, Megan Richardson, Stefano Rodotà, Jamie Smith, and Nigel Waters. None should be indicted as a co-defendant for the transgressions I have committed here and elsewhere.

As always, members of Oxford University Press have been congenial collaborators in this project. I am especially grateful to Andrea Keegan, Emma Marchant, Keira Dickinson, Kerstin Demata, and Deborah Protheroe. Not for the first time, Kartiga Ramalingam and her team at SPI have done a superb job of transforming my text and images into this handsome volume.

Since putting the finishing touches to the manuscript – and even while reading the proofs – accounts of innumerable invasions relentlessly proliferated. Reader, be warned: the topic of the book in your hands is highly volatile. Fresh challenges to personal privacy lie in wait. The quest to protect and preserve this indispensable democratic ideal demands vigilance and resolve.

Raymond Wacks

# List of Illustrations

# Chapter 1
# **The assault**

Once upon a time, passengers boarded an aircraft without a search. Hacking described a cough – probably caused by a virus; and cookies were to be eaten rather than feared.

You are being watched. The ubiquity of Big Brother no longer shocks. 'Low-tech' collection of transactional data in both the public and private sector has become commonplace. In addition to the routine surveillance by CCTV in public places, the monitoring of mobile telephones, the workplace, vehicles, electronic communications, and online activity has swiftly become widespread in most advanced societies.

Privacy in its broadest sense extends beyond these sorts of intrusions whose principal pursuit is personal information. It would include a multiplicity of incursions into the private domain – especially by the government – captured in Warren and Brandeis's phrase 'the right to be let alone'. This comprehensive notion, redolent of the celebrated 17th-century declaration by Sir Edward Coke that 'a man's house is his castle', embraces a wide range of invasions that encroach not only upon 'spatial' and 'locational' privacy, but also interfere with 'decisional' matters often of a moral character such as abortion, contraception, and sexual preference.

In the case of surveillance, a moment's reflection will reveal some of its many ironies – and difficulties. Its nature – and our reaction to it – is neither straightforward nor obvious. Is 'Big Brother is Watching You' a threat, a statement of fact, or merely mendacious intimidation? Does it make any difference? Is it the knowledge that I am being observed by, say, a CCTV camera, that violates my privacy? What if the camera is a (now widely available) imitation that credibly simulates the action of the genuine article: flashing light, probing lens, menacing swing? Nothing is recorded, but I am unaware of its innocence. What is my objection? Or suppose the camera is real, but faulty – and no images are made, stored, or used? My actions have not been monitored, yet subjectively my equanimity has been disturbed. The mere presence of a device that appears to be observing and recording my behaviour is surely tantamount to the reality of my unease.

In other words, it is the *belief* that I am being watched that is my grievance. It is immaterial whether I am in fact the subject of surveillance. My objection is therefore not that I am being observed – for I am not – but the possibility that I may be.

In this respect, being watched by a visible CCTV camera differs from that other indispensable instrument of the spy: the electronic listening device. When my room or office is bugged, or my telephone is tapped, I am – by definition – usually oblivious to this infringement of my privacy. Yet my ignorance does not, of course, render the practice inoffensive. Unlike the case of the fake or non-functioning camera, however, I *have* been subjected to surveillance: my private conversations have been recorded or intercepted, albeit unconsciously. The same would be true of the surreptitious interception of my correspondence: email or snail mail.

In the former case, no personal information has been captured; in the latter, it has, but I may never know. Both practices are subsumed in the category of 'intrusion', yet each exhibits a distinctive apprehension. Indeed, the more one examines this

1. The English Utilitarian Jeremy Bentham designed a prison that facilitates the surreptitious observation of inmates. The term 'panopticon' is used metaphorically in a pejorative sense to describe the monitoring of individuals' personal information, especially online

(neglected) problem, the less cohesive the subject of 'intrusion' becomes. Each activity requires a separate analysis; each entails a discrete set of concerns, though they are united in a general anxiety that one's society may be approaching, or already displays features of, the Orwellian horror of relentless scrutiny.

The question is fundamentally one of perception and its consequences. Although my conviction that I am being monitored by CCTV is based on palpable evidence, and my ignorance of the interception of my correspondence or conversations is plainly not, the discomfort is similar. In both cases, it is the distasteful recognition that one needs to adjust one's behaviour – on the assumption that one's words or deeds are being monitored. During the darkest years of repression in apartheid South Africa, for example, the telephones of anti-government activists were routinely tapped by the security services. One's conversations were therefore conducted with circumspection and trepidation. This inevitably rendered dialogue stilted and unnatural. It is this requirement to adapt or adjust one's behaviour in public (in the case of CCTV) or in private (on the telephone, in one's home, or online) that is the disquieting result of a state that fails properly to regulate the exercise of surveillance.

The increasing use of such surveillance in the workplace, for instance, is changing not only the character of that environment, but also the very nature of what we do and how we do it. The knowledge that our activities are, or even may be, monitored undermines our psychological and emotional autonomy:

> Free conversation is often characterized by exaggeration, obscenity, agreeable falsehoods, and the expression of antisocial desires or views not intended to be taken seriously. The unedited quality of conversation is essential if it is to preserve its intimate, personal and informal character.

Indeed, the slide towards electronic supervision may fundamentally alter our relationships and our identity. In such a world, employees are arguably less likely to execute their duties effectively. If that occurs, the snooping employer will, in the end, secure the precise opposite of what he hopes to achieve.

## Wiretapping

Both landlines and mobile phones are easy prey to the eavesdropper. In the case of the former, the connection is simply a long circuit comprising a pair of copper wires that form a loop. The circuit carrying your conversation flows out of your home through numerous switching stations between you and the instrument on the other end. At any point a snoop can attach a new load to the circuit board, much in the way one plugs in an additional appliance into an extension cord. In the case of wiretapping, that load is a mechanism that converts the electrical circuit back into the sound of your conversation. The chief shortcoming of this primitive form of interception is that the spy needs to know when the subject is going to use the phone. He needs to be at his post to listen in.

A less inconvenient and more sophisticated method is to install a recording device on the line. Like an answering machine, it picks ups the electrical signal from the telephone line and encodes it as magnetic pulses on audiotape. The disadvantage of this method is that the intruder needs to keep the recorder running continuously in order to monitor any conversations. Few cassettes are large enough. Hence a voice-activated recorder provides a more practical alternative. But here too the tape is unlikely to endure long enough to capture the subject's conversations.

The obvious answer is a bug that receives audio information and broadcasts it using radio waves. Bugs normally have diminutive microphones that pick up sound waves directly. The current is sent to a radio transmitter that conveys a signal that varies with the current. The spy sets up a radio receiver in the vicinity that picks up

Outside lines can be tapped directly with a hardwired tap.

Bugs can be installed in the wall socket, the handset or anywhere along the phone line.

A simple recording device can be attached to a phone line, but it can be easily detected.

With the right equipment, bugs and wireless communications can be monitored from a distance.

©2006 Howstuffworks

Privacy

**2. Tapping a telephone is a fairly simple operation**

this signal and transmits it to a speaker or encodes it on a tape. A bug with a microphone is especially valuable since it will hear any conversation in the room, regardless of whether the subject is on the phone. A conventional wiretapping bug, however, can operate without its own microphone, since the telephone has one. All the wiretapper needs to do is to connect the bug anywhere along the phone line, since it receives the electrical current directly. Normally, the spy will connect the bug to the wires inside the telephone.

This is the classic approach. It obviates the need for the spy to revisit the site; his recording equipment may be concealed in a van that typically is parked outside the victim's home or office.

Tapping mobile phones requires the interception of radio signals carried from and to the handsets, and converting them back into sound. The analogue mobile phones of the 1990s were susceptible to easy interception, but their contemporary digital counterparts are much less vulnerable. To read the signals, the digital computer bits need to be converted into sound – a fairly complex and expensive operation. But mobile phone calls may be intercepted at the mobile operator's servers, or on a fixed-line section that carries encrypted voice data for wireless communication.

When you call someone on your mobile phone, your voice is digitized and sent to the nearest base station. It transmits it to another base station adjacent to the recipient's via the mobile carrier's switch operators. Between the base stations, transmission of voice data is effected on landlines, as occurs in the case of fixed-line phone calls. It seems that if an eavesdropper listens to such calls over the landline connection segment, mobile phones are not dissimilar to conventional phones – and as vulnerable.

## The privacy prognosis

The future of surveillance seems daunting. It promises more sophisticated and alarming intrusions into our private lives, including the greater use of biometrics, and sense-enhanced searches such as satellite monitoring, penetrating walls and clothing, and 'smart dust' devices – minuscule wireless micro-electromechanical sensors (MEMS) that can detect everything from light to vibrations. These so-called 'motes' – as tiny as a grain of sand – would collect data that could be sent via two-way band radio between motes up to 1,000 feet away.

As cyberspace becomes an increasingly perilous domain, we learn daily of new, disquieting assaults on its citizens. This slide towards pervasive surveillance coincides with the mounting fears, expressed well before 11 September 2001, about the disconcerting capacity of the new technology to undermine our liberty. Reports of the fragility of privacy have been sounded for at least a century. But in the last decade they have assumed a more urgent form. And here lies a paradox. On the one hand, recent advances in the power of computers have been decried as the nemesis of whatever vestiges of our privacy still survive. On the other, the Internet is acclaimed as a Utopia. When clichés contend, it is imprudent to expect sensible resolutions of the problems they embody, but between these two exaggerated claims, something resembling the truth probably resides. In respect of the future of privacy at least, there can be little doubt that the questions are changing before our eyes. And if, in the flat-footed domain of atoms, we have achieved only limited success in protecting individuals against the depredations of surveillance, how much better the prospects in our brave new binary world?

When our security is under siege, so – inevitably – is our liberty. A world in which our every movement is observed erodes the very freedom this snooping is often calculated to protect. Naturally, we need to ensure that the social costs of the means employed to enhance security do not outweigh the benefits. Thus, one unsurprising consequence of the installation of CCTV in car parks, shopping centres, airports, and other public places is the displacement of crime; offenders simply go somewhere else. And, apart from the doors this intrusion opens to totalitarianism, a surveillance society can easily generate a climate of mistrust and suspicion, a reduction in the respect for law and those who enforce it, and an intensification of prosecution of offences that are susceptible to easy detection and proof.

Other developments have comprehensively altered basic features of the legal landscape. The law has been profoundly affected and challenged by countless other advances in technology. Computer fraud, identity theft, and other 'cyber crimes' are touched on below.

Developments in biotechnology such as cloning, stem cell research, and genetic engineering provoke thorny ethical questions and confront traditional legal concepts. Proposals to introduce identity cards and biometrics have attracted strong objections in several jurisdictions. The nature of criminal trials has been transformed by the use of both DNA and CCTV evidence.

Orwellian supervision already appears to be alive and well in several countries. Britain, for example, boasts more than 4 million CCTV

3. **The ubiquity of CCTV cameras may diminish their efficacy**

cameras in public places: roughly one for every 14 inhabitants. It also possesses the world's largest DNA database, comprising some 5.3 million DNA samples. The temptation to install CCTV cameras by both the public and private sector is not easy to resist. Data-protection law (discussed in Chapter 5) ostensibly controls its use, but such regulation has not proved especially effective. A radical solution, adopted in Denmark, is to prohibit their use, subject to certain exceptions such as in petrol stations. The law in Sweden, France, and Holland is more stringent than in the United Kingdom. These countries adopt a licensing system, and the law requires that warning signs be placed on the periphery of the zone monitored. German law has a similar requirement.

## Biometrics

We are all unique. Your fingerprint is a 'biometric': the measurement of biological information. Fingerprints have long been used as a means of linking an individual to a crime, but they provide also a practical method of privacy protection: instead of logging into your computer with a (not always safe) password, increasing use is being made of fingerprint readers as a considerably more secure entry point. We are likely to see greater use of fingerprint readers at supermarket checkouts and ATMs.

There is no perfect biometric, but the ideal is to find a unique personal attribute that is immutable or, at least, unlikely to change over time. A measurement of this characteristic is then employed as a means of identifying the individual in question. Typically, several samples of the biometric are provided by the subject; they are digitized and stored on a database. The biometric may then be used either to identify the subject by matching his or her data against that of a number of other individuals' biometrics, or to validate the identity of a single subject.

In order to counter the threat of terrorism, the future will unquestionably witness an increased use of biometrics. This includes a number of measures of human physiography as well as DNA. Among the following examples of characteristics on which biometric technologies can be based are one's appearance (supported by still images), e.g., descriptions used in passports, such as height, weight, colour of skin, hair, and eyes, visible physical markings, gender, race, facial hair, wearing of glasses; natural physiography, e.g., skull measurements, teeth and skeletal injuries, thumbprint, fingerprint sets, handprints, iris and retinal scans, earlobe capillary patterns, hand geometry; biodynamics, e.g., the manner in which one's signature is written, statistically analysed voice characteristics, keystroke dynamics, particularly login-ID and password; social behaviour (supported by video-film), e.g., habituated body signals, general voice characteristics, style of speech, visible handicaps; imposed physical characteristics, e.g., dog-tags, collars, bracelets and anklets, bar-codes, embedded microchips, and transponders.

The fear is that in authoritarian countries, biometrics may be imposed on the public. Biometrics providers will thrive by selling their technology to repressive governments, and establish a foothold in relatively free countries by seeking soft targets; they

## The limits of biometrics

One identification option often mentioned is to implant microchips into people to store and broadcast identity, but we cannot rule out the possibility that the chip could be surgically removed and replaced, or that the information could be changed via remote access. Even if we take a DNA sample from a baby when it is still attached to its mother, there is still the possibility of substituting another sample on its journey to the lab for analysis. There is no absolutely foolproof method of securing the identity of a person, even via the most accurate of biometrics.

K. O'Hara and N. Shadbolt, *The Spy in the Coffee Machine* (Oneworld, 2008), pp. 68–9 may start with animals or with captive populations such as the frail, the poor, the old, prisoners, employees, and so on. A less gloomy scenario is that societies will recognize the gravity of the threat and enforce constraints on technologies and their use. This would require public support and the courage of elected representatives who will need to resist pressure both from large corporations and the national security and law enforcement authorities that invoke the bogeymen of terrorism, illegal immigration, and domestic 'law and order' to justify the implementation of this technology.

## The Internet

Online activity is especially vulnerable to attack. The artillery of malicious software (or 'malware') includes viruses, worms, Trojan horses, spyware, 'phishing', 'bots', 'zombies', bugs, and exploits.

A virus is a block of code that introduces copies of itself into other programs. It normally carries a payload, which may have only nuisance value, though in many cases the consequences are serious. In order to evade early detection, viruses may delay the performance of functions other than replication. A worm generates copies of itself over networks without infecting other programs. A Trojan horse is a program that appears to carry out a positive task (and sometimes does so), but is often nasty, for instance, keystroke recorders embedded in utilities.

4. **Surfing is beset with hazards**

Spyware is software – often hidden within an email attachment – that secretly harvests data within a device about its user, or applications made by the device. These are passed on to another party. The data may include the user's browsing history, log individual keystrokes (to obtain passwords), monitor user behaviour for consumer marketing purposes (so-called 'adware'), or observe the use of copyrighted works. 'Phishing' normally takes the form of an email message that appears to emanate from a trusted institution such as a bank. It seeks to entice the addressee into divulging sensitive data such as a password or credit card details. The messages are normally highly implausible – replete with spelling mistakes and other obvious defects – yet this manifest deceit manages to dupe an extraordinarily high number of recipients.

Some malware filches personal data or transforms your computer into a 'bot' – one which is remotely controlled by a third party. A 'bot' may be employed to collect email addresses, send spam, or mount attacks on corporate websites. Another form of attack is 'Denial of Service' (DoS), which uses a swarm of 'bots' or 'zombies' to inundate company websites with bogus data requests. A 'zombie' creates numerous processors dotted around the Internet under central or timed control (hence 'zombies'). An attack will pursue a website until it has been taken offline. This may endure for several days, incurring considerable costs to the victim company. They are typically accompanied by demands for money.

Bugs are errors in software – particularly Microsoft Windows – that may render the user's system vulnerable to attack by so-called 'crackers'. Microsoft normally responds by issuing a patch for downloading – until the next bug materializes. An 'exploit' is an attack on a particular vulnerability. Standard techniques are supported by established guidelines and programming code that circulate on the Internet.

It was reported in early 2009 that police in the European Union have been encouraged to expand the implementation of a rarely used power of intrusion – without warrant. This will permit police across Europe to hack into private computers when an officer believes that such a 'remote search' is proportionate and necessary to prevent or detect serious crime (one which attracts a prison sentence of more than three years). This could be achieved in a number of ways, including the attachment of a virus to an email message which, if opened, would covertly activate the remote search facility.

## Cookies

These are data that the website servers transmit to the visitor's browser and are stored on his or her computer. They enable the website to recognize the visitor's computer as one with which it has previously interacted, and to remember details of the earlier transaction, including search words, and the amount of time spent reading certain pages. In other words, cookie technology enables a website – by default – furtively to put its own identifier into my PC permanently in order track my online conduct.

And cookies can endure; they may show an extensive list of each website visited during a particular period. Moreover, the text of the cookie file may reveal personal data previously provided. Websites such as Amazon.com justify this practice by claiming that it assists and improves the shopping experience by informing customers of books which, on the basis of their browsing behaviour, they might otherwise neglect to buy. But this gives rise to the obvious danger that my identity may be misrepresented by a concentration on tangential segments of my surfing or, on the other hand, personal data harvested from a variety of sources may be assembled to create a comprehensive lifestyle profile.

5. No one, it would seem, is immune to hacking

## Hacking

Hackers were once regarded as innocuous 'cyber-snoops' who adhered to a slightly self-indulgent, but quasi-ethical, code dictating that one ought not to purloin data, but merely report holes in the victim's system (see box). They were, as Lessig puts it, 'a bit more invasive than a security guard, who checks office doors to make sure they are locked ... (He) not only checked the locks but let himself in, took a quick peek around, and left a cute (or sarcastic) note saying, in effect, "Hey, stupid, you left your door open."'

While this laid-back culture eventually attracted the interest of law-enforcement authorities – who secured legislation against it – the practice continues to produce headaches. According to Simon Church of VeriSign, the online auction sites that criminals use to sell user details, are merely the beginning. He anticipates that

## The (dubious) joy of hacking

Being a hacker is lots of fun, but it's a kind of fun that takes lots of effort. The effort takes motivation. Successful athletes get their motivation from a kind of physical delight in making their bodies perform, in pushing themselves past their own physical limits. Similarly, to be a hacker you have to get a basic thrill from solving problems, sharpening your skills, and exercising your intelligence. If you aren't the kind of person that feels this way naturally, you'll need to become one in order to make it as a hacker. Otherwise you'll find your hacking energy is sapped by distractions like sex, money, and social approval . . . To behave like a hacker, you have to believe that the thinking time of other hackers is precious – so much so that it's almost a moral duty for you to share information, solve problems and then give the solutions away just so other hackers can solve *new* problems instead of having to perpetually re-address old ones . . . Hackers (and creative people in general) should never be bored or have to drudge at stupid repetitive work, because when this happens it means they aren't doing what only they can do – solve new problems. This wastefulness hurts everybody. Therefore boredom and drudgery are not just unpleasant but actually evil . . . Hackers are naturally anti-authoritarian. Anyone who can give you orders can stop you from solving whatever problem you're being fascinated by – and, given the way authoritarian minds work, will generally find some appallingly stupid reason to do so. So the authoritarian attitude has to be fought wherever you find it, lest it smother you and other hackers . . . To be a hacker, you have to develop some of these attitudes. But copping an attitude alone won't make you a hacker, any more than it will make you a champion athlete or a rock star. Becoming a hacker will take intelligence, practice, dedication, and hard work . . . If you revere competence, you'll enjoy developing it in yourself – the hard work and dedication will become a kind of intense play rather than drudgery. That attitude is vital to becoming a hacker.

Eric Steven Raymond, *How to Become a Hacker*, http://www.catb.org/~esr/faqs/ hacker-howto.html 'mashup' sites that combine different databases could be converted to criminal use. 'Imagine if a hacker put together information he'd harvested from a travel company's database with Google Maps. He could provide a tech-savvy burglar with the driving directions of how to get to your empty house the minute you go on holiday.'

## Identity theft

The appropriation of an individual's personal information to commit fraud or to impersonate him or her is an escalating problem, costing billions of dollars a year. In 2007, a survey by the United States Federal Trade Commission found that in 2005, a total of 3.7% of survey participants indicated that they had been victims of identity theft. This result suggests that approximately 8.3 million American suffered some form of identity theft in that year, and 10% of all victims reported out-of-pocket expenses of $1,200 or more. The same percentage spent at least 55 hours resolving their problems. The top 5% of victims spent at least 130 hours. The estimate of total losses from identity theft in the 2006 survey amounted to $15.6 billion.

The practice normally involves at least three persons: the victim, the impostor, and a credit institution that establishes a new account for the impostor in the victim's name. This may include a credit card, utilities service, or even a mortgage.

Identity theft assumes a number of forms. Potentially the most harmful comprise credit card fraud (in which an account number is stolen in order to make unauthorized charges), new account fraud (where the impostor initiates an account or 'tradeline' in the victim's name; the offence may be undiscovered until the victim applies for credit), identity cloning (where the impostor masquerades as the victim), and criminal identity theft (in which the impostor, masquerading as the victim, is arrested for some offence, or is fined for a violation of the law).

Part of the responsibility must be laid at the door of the financial services industry itself. Their lax security methods in granting credit and facilitating electronic payment subordinates security to convenience.

## Identity cards

At first blush, a compulsory ID card that contains the holder's key personal information would appear to be a panacea for the multiple problems of identity theft, tax and welfare fraud, illegal immigration, and, of course, terrorism. Yet, quite apart from their actual efficacy in curbing harmful activities, their establishment inevitably invokes fervent hostility, especially from privacy advocates, and particularly in common law jurisdictions such as the United Kingdom, Australia, Canada, the United States, Ireland, and New Zealand where attempts to introduce them have so far been unsuccessful. Resistance has been intense also in Scandinavian countries. Cultural forces clearly operate against the notion that an individual is required to carry 'papers'. In Britain, for example, there is a deep-seated objection to any compulsion to prove one's democratic right to exist!

Compulsory ID cards do, however, exist in various forms in about 100 countries, and there is considerably less opposition to the use of various types of mandatory ID cards in Europe and Asia. Eleven European Union members, including France, Germany, Spain, Portugal, Belgium, Greece, and Luxembourg, use them. In Asia, the Hong Kong experience is instructive. ID cards have been used since 1945 – principally (or, at least, ostensibly) to control the influx of illegal immigrants from mainland China. And it is undoubtedly the case that the vast majority of Hong Kong residents are perfectly insouciant about both the requirement to carry the card at all times and the personal data that it holds. Indeed, it has become a highly convenient means by which to substantiate one's identity for purposes of buying theatre tickets, booking a restaurant, and the like.

Recently the Hong Kong government 'upgraded' the cards into what are now styled 'identity smart cards' with a chip containing, *inter alia*, the holder's particulars of birth, nationality, address, marital status, occupation, and details of any spouse or children. To obtain the card, the law requires residents to be photographed and fingerprinted. The government claims that there are a number of benefits that accrue from the use of the smart card, including greater security (data engraved into different layers of the card and held in the chip can prevent lost or stolen identity cards from being altered or used by others); convenience (with the capacity of multi-applications, such as e-certificate and library card functions, the holder may use one card for various functions); 'quality service' (card holders will enjoy various kinds of public services online); and more convenient travel (the thumbprint templates stored in the chip facilitate speedy immigration clearance via the Automated Passenger Clearance System and the Automated Vehicle Clearance System).

To allay fears of the misuse of the data, the government maintains that only minimal data are stored in the RFID (radio frequency identification) chip. More sensitive personal information is kept at back-end computer systems. Data for different applications are segregated. All the non-immigration applications are voluntary. The collection, storage, use, and release of data must comply with, amongst other legislation, the Personal Data (Privacy) Ordinance. Only authorized departments have access to the relevant database; there is no sharing of databases among government departments. Cardholders may view data on the card through smart identity card readers installed at immigration self-service kiosks after their identities have been authenticated. Privacy Impact Assessments (PIA) are conducted at different stages of the Smart Identity Card

## Twelve arguments against ID cards

1. They won't stop crime.
2. They won't stop welfare fraud.
3. They will not stop illegal immigration.
4. They will facilitate discrimination.
5. They will create an unwarranted increase in police powers.
6. They will become an internal passport.
7. A 'voluntary' card will become compulsory.
8. The cost will be unacceptable.
9. The loss of a card will cause great distress and inconvenience.
10. A card will imperil the privacy of personal information.
11. The card will entrench criminality and institutionalize false identity.
12. They will compromise national identity and personal integrity.

Simon Davies, *Big Brother* (Pan Books, 1996), pp. 139–51

Project. Legislative amendments have been enacted to enhance data privacy protection.

This sounds reassuring, and the attractions of greater efficiency, equity, and convenience are not to be lightly dismissed. But, as with the proposed ID card in Britain, these virtues must be balanced against the very real prospect of 'function creep', error, confidentiality, and identity theft. The temptation of any government bureaucracy to use the data for a variety of purposes, to share information between departments, and to merge databases may be irresistible. Nor is it obvious that the fraudster or terrorist will be thwarted by even the most sophisticated ID card.

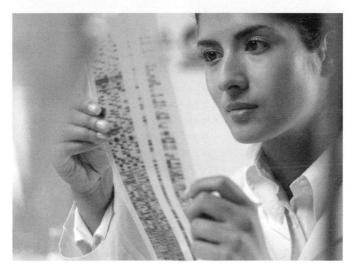

**6. The various uses to which DNA is put pose considerable risks to personal privacy**

## DNA databases

The growing use of DNA evidence in the detection of crime has generated a need for a database of samples to determine whether an individual's profile matches that of a suspect. The DNA database in England and Wales (with its 5.3 million profiles, representing 9% of the population) may be the largest anywhere. It includes DNA samples and fingerprints of almost a million suspects who are never prosecuted or who are subsequently acquitted. It is hardly surprising that innocent persons should feel aggrieved by the retention of their genetic information; the potential for misuse is not a trivial matter. This dismal prospect led two such individuals to request that their profiles be expunged following their walking free. Unable to convince the English courts, they appealed to the European Court of Human Rights, which, at the end of 2008, unanimously decided that their right to privacy had been violated.

## The spy in your bed

Computers are getting smaller and smaller and can be made of, or fitted into, many new and interesting materials. The possibilities are endless, but so are the dangers. For instance, the field of electronic textiles or 'washable computing' provides all sorts of fascinating futures. Fabrics that can monitor vital signs, generate heat or act as switches suggest limitless possibilities, from the ridiculous – clothes that change colour constantly – to the useful – a jacket that recharges your mobile phone. Textronic's 'textro-polymer' is made of fibres that change their resistance as they are deformed, stretched, and so can detect pressure. Very handy – but imagine a bedsheet that was able to detect, and broadcast, the number of people lying on it.

K. O'Hara and N. Shadbolt, *The Spy in the Coffee Machine* (Oneworld, 2008), p. 9

Other jurisdictions tend to destroy a DNA profile when a suspect is acquitted. In Norway and Germany, for example, a sample may be kept permanently only with the approval of a court. In Sweden, only the profiles of convicted offenders who have served custodial sentences of more than two years may be retained. The United States permits the FBI to take DNA samples on arrest, but they can be destroyed on request should no charges be laid or if the suspect is acquitted. Among the 40 or so states that have DNA databases, only California permits permanent storage of profiles of individuals charged but then cleared.

It has been suggested that, to avoid discrimination against certain sectors of the population (such as black males), everybody's DNA should be collected and held in the database. This drastic proposal is unlikely to attract general support. What is clear, however, is that to maintain the integrity of the system and protect privacy, the vulnerability of such sensitive genetic data requires stringent regulation.

# Repelling the attacks

Privacy-enhancing technologies (PETs) seek to protect privacy by eliminating or reducing personal data or by preventing unnecessary or undesired processing of personal data without compromising the operation of the data system. Originally they took the form of 'pseudonymization tools': software that allows individuals to withhold their true identity from operating electronic systems, and only reveal it when absolutely essential. These technologies help to reduce the amount of data collected about an individual. Their efficacy, however, depends largely on the integrity of those who have the power to revoke or nullify the shield of the pseudonym. Unhappily, governments cannot always be trusted.

Instead of pseudonymity, stronger PETs afford the tougher armour of anonymity that denies the ability of governments and corporations to link data with an identified individual. This is normally achieved by a succession of intermediary-operated services. Each intermediary knows the identities of the intermediaries next to it in the chain, but has insufficient information to facilitate the identification of the previous and succeeding intermediaries. It cannot trace the communication to the originator, or forward it to the eventual recipient.

These PETs include anonymous re-mailers, web-surfing measures, and David Chaum's payer-anonymous electronic cash (e-cash) or *Digicash* which employs a blinding technique that sends randomly encrypted data to my bank which then validates them (through the use of some sort of digital money) and returns the data to my hard disk. Only a serial number is provided: the recipient does not know (and does not need to know) the source of the payment. This process affords an even more powerful safeguard of anonymity. It has considerable potential in electronic copyright management systems (ECMS) with projects such as CITED (Copyright in Transmitted Electronic Documents) and COPICAT, being developed by the European Commission ESPIRIT programme. Full texts of copyrighted works are being downloaded and marketed without the owner's consent or royalty being paid. These projects seek technological solutions by which users could be charged for their use of such material. This 'tracking' of users poses an obvious privacy danger: my reading, listening, or viewing habits may be stored, and access to them obtained, for potentially sinister or harmful purposes. Blind signatures seem to be a relatively simple means by which to anonymize users.

Anonymity is an important democratic value. Even in a pre-electronic age, it facilitates participation in the political process which an individual may otherwise wish to spurn. Indeed, the United States Supreme Court has held that the First Amendment protects the right to anonymous speech. There are numerous reasons why I may wish to conceal my identity behind a pseudonym or achieve anonymity in some other way. On the Internet, I may want to be openly anonymous but conduct a conversation (with either known or anonymous identities) using an anonymous remailer. I may even wish no one to know the identity of the recipient of my email. And I may not want anyone to know to which newsgroups I belong or which websites I have visited.

There are, moreover, obvious personal and political benefits of anonymity for whistleblowers, victims of abuse, and those requiring help of various kinds. Equally, (as always?), such liberties may also shield criminal activities, though the right to anonymous speech would not extend to unlawful speech. Anonymity enjoys a unique relationship with both privacy and free speech. The opportunities for anonymity afforded by the Internet are substantial; we are probably only on the brink of discovering its potential in both spheres. It raises (somewhat disquieting) questions about the very question of who we are: our identity.

The use of strong encryption to protect the security of communications has been met by resistance (notably in the United

States and France) and by proposals either to prohibit encryption altogether, or, through means such as public key escrow, to preserve the power to intercept messages. The battle has been joined between law enforcers and cryptographers; it is likely to be protracted, especially since enthusiastic would be too meek a word to describe the manner in which the culture of strong encryption has been embraced by ordinary computer users – given that Phil Zimmerman's encryption software, PGP ('Pretty Good Privacy'), may be generated in less than five minutes, and is freely available on the Internet.

A central feature of modern cryptography is that of the 'public key'. A lock-and-key approach is adopted in respect of telecommunications security. The lock is a public key which a user may transmit to recipients. To unlock the message, the recipient uses a personal encryption code or 'private key'. Public key encryption significantly increases the availability of encryption/identification, for the dual key system allows the encryption key to be made available to potential communicants while keeping the decryption key secret. It permits, for instance, a bank to make its public key available to several customers, without their being able to read each others' encrypted messages.

Technological solutions are especially useful in concealing the identity of the individual. Weak forms of digital identities are already widely used in the form of bank account and social security numbers. They provide only limited protection, for it is a simple matter to match them with the person they represent. The advent of smart cards that generate changing pseudo-identities will facilitate genuine transactional anonymity. 'Blinding' or 'blind signatures' and 'digital signatures' will significantly enhance the protection of privacy. A digital signature is a unique 'key' which provides, if anything, stronger authentication than my written signature. A public key system involves two keys, one public and the other private. The advantage of a public key system is that if you are able to decrypt the message, you know that it could only have been created by the sender.

The paramount question is: is my identity *genuinely required* for the act or transaction concerned? It is here that data-protection principles, discussed in Chapter 5, come into play.

## P3P

A significant development in privacy policy management systems are technologies that permit a user to make informed choices about their browsing based on his or her personal privacy preferences. The best known of these protocols is the Platform for Privacy Preferences (P3P) developed by the World Wide Web Consortium (W3C). It allows websites to make machine-readable versions of their privacy policies, thereby enabling users whose browsers are equipped with P3P readers to have their specified privacy preferences automatically compared to the website's privacy policy. This will state clearly what information the site collects and what it will do with it. Users are then notified if the website policy does not match their preferences.

One of the leading privacy advocate organizations, the Electronic Privacy Information Center (EPIC) is, however, unconvinced. Dubbing it 'Pretty Poor Privacy', it complains that P3P fails to comply with baseline standards for privacy protection:

> It is a complex and confusing protocol that will make it more difficult for Internet users to protect their privacy. P3P also fails to address many of the privacy problems specifically associated with the Internet.

EPIC contends that good privacy standards are better built on fair information practices and genuine PETs that minimize or eliminate the collection of personally identifiable information:

Simple, predictable rules for the collection and use of personal information will also support consumer trust and confidence. P3P, on the other hand, is likely to undermine public confidence in Internet privacy.

7. **The escalating use of RFID technology poses numerous threats to privacy**

## RFID

The technology of radio frequency identification emerged as a means of inventory control to replace barcodes. An RFID system consists of three elements: a minuscule chip on each consumer item (an RFID tag) that stores a unique product identifier; an RFID reader; and a computer system attached to the reader having access to an inventory control database. The database contains extensive product information, including the contents, origin, and manufacturing history of the product. Assigning a tag to a product also discloses its location, rate and place of sale, and, in the case of transport companies, its progress. It has applications in recalling faulty or dangerous merchandise, tracing stolen property, preventing counterfeit, and providing an audit trail to thwart corruption.

The potential of RFID is huge, and it is increasingly being used for 'contactless' payment cards, passports, and the monitoring of luggage, library books, and pets. There is no reason why humans could not be microchipped – like our dogs. It could assist the identification of Alzheimer's patients who go astray. Combining RFID and wireless fidelity networks (Wi-Fi) could facilitate real-time tracking of objects or people inside a wireless network, such as a hospital. The privacy concern is that the acceptance of these benign applications may initiate less benevolent uses; there are likely to be calls for sex offenders, prisoners, illegal immigrants, and other 'undesirables' to be tagged.

There is also the fear that if RFID data may be aggregated with other data (for example, information stored in credit or loyalty cards) – to match product data with personal information – this could allow comprehensive personal profiles of consumers to be assembled. Moreover, an increase in the use of RFID in public places, and homes and businesses, could portend an enlargement of the surveillance society. For example, my car has an RFID affixed to the windscreen that automatically deducts the toll from my bank account. The fact that it has just passed through the toll station at Pisa may be useful to a party interested in my movements. There is plainly a need for sophisticated PETs here.

## Global positioning system

Satellite signals are used by GPS to establish location. GPS chips are now common in vehicle navigation systems and mobile phones. It is possible to augment the data generated from GPS by their assimilation into databases and aggregation with other information to create geographic information systems (GIS). In order to make or receive calls, mobile phones communicate their location to a base station. In effect, therefore, they broadcast the user's location every few minutes.

Services such as Loki triangulate position using wireless signals, allowing the user to obtain local weather reports, find nearby restaurants, cinemas, or shops, or share their location with friends. According to its website, 'as you travel around, MyLoki can automatically let your friends know where you are using your favourite platform – Facebook, RSS Feeds, or badges for your blog or even Twitter'. It claims to protect privacy by refraining from the collection of personal information.

## Genetic information

The ability to explore our genetic structure poses a number of privacy problems, not least the extent to which a doctor's duty to preserve patient confidentiality, enshrined in the Hippocratic Oath, adequately safeguards this sensitive information against disclosure. It raises too the intractable problem of the subject's blood relatives – and even partners and spouses – whose interest in learning of the data is far from trivial.

The challenges posed by these – and other – intrusions cannot be underestimated. How have we arrived at this situation? The next chapter attempts to provide an answer.

# Chapter 2
# **An enduring value**

While much of our contemporary disquiet about privacy tends to spring from the malevolent capacity of technology, the yearning for a private realm long precedes the Brave New World of bits and bytes, of electronic surveillance, and CCTV. Indeed, anthropologists have demonstrated that there is a near-universal desire for individual and group privacy in primitive societies, and that this is reflected in appropriate social norms. Moreover, we are not alone in seeking refuge from the crowd. Animals too need privacy.

## What is privacy?

At the most general level, the idea of privacy embraces the desire to be left alone, free to be ourselves – uninhibited and unconstrained by the prying of others. This extends beyond snooping and unsolicited publicity to intrusions upon the 'space' we need to make intimate, personal decisions without the intrusion of the state. Thus 'privacy' is frequently employed to describe a zone demarcated as 'private' in which, for example, a woman exercises a choice as to whether she wishes to have an abortion, or an individual is free to express his or her sexuality. Debates about privacy are therefore often entangled with contentious moral

## Privacy and animals

Man likes to think that his desire for privacy is distinctively human, a function of his unique ethical, intellectual, and artistic needs. Yet studies of animal behaviour and social organization suggest that man's need for privacy may well be rooted in his animal origins, and that men and animals share several basic mechanisms for claiming privacy among their own fellows... Studies of territoriality have even shattered the romantic notion that when robins sing or monkeys shriek, it is solely for the 'animal joy of life'. Actually, it is often a defiant cry for privacy... One basic finding of animal studies is that virtually all animals seek periods of individual seclusion or small-group intimacy... (T)he animal's struggle to achieve a balance between privacy and participation provides one of the basic processes of animal life. In this sense, the quest for privacy is not restricted to man alone, but arises in the biological and social processes of all life.

Alan Westin, *Privacy and Freedom* (The Bodley Head, 1967), pp. 8–11

questions, including the use of contraception and the right to pornography.

In any event, it is clear that at the core of our concern to protect privacy lies a conception of the individual's relationship with society. Once we acknowledge a separation between the public and the private domain, we assume a community in which not only does such a division make sense, but also an institutional structure that makes possible an account of this sort. In other words, to postulate the 'private' presupposes the 'public'.

Over the last century or so, participation in the public realm – in society – has undergone steady erosion. We are more self-centred. Our postmodern psychological preoccupation with 'being in touch with' our feelings, as the sociologist Richard Sennett vividly demonstrates, devastated the prospect of a genuine political community. Paradoxically, excessive intimacy has destroyed it: 'The closer people come, the less social, the more painful, the more fratricidal their relations.'

In fact, the Greeks regarded a life spent in the privacy of 'one's own' (*idion*) as, by definition, 'idiotic'. Similarly, the Romans perceived privacy as merely a temporary refuge from the life of the *res publica*. This is well described by Hannah Arendt:

> In ancient feeling the private trait of privacy, indicated in the word itself, was all-important; it meant literally a state of being deprived of something, and even of the highest and most human of man's capacities. A man who lived only a private life, who like the slave was not permitted to enter the public realm, or like the barbarian had chosen not to establish such a realm, was not fully human.

Only in the late Roman Empire can one discern the initial stages of the recognition of privacy as a zone of intimacy.

As one might expect, ancient and primitive societies display diverse attitudes to privacy. In his seminal study *Privacy Rights: Moral and Legal Foundations*, Barrington Moore examined the state of privacy in a number of early communities, including classical Athens, Jewish society as revealed in the Old Testament, and ancient China. In the case of China, he illustrates how the Confucian distinction between the separate realms of the state (public) and the family (private), as well as early texts on courtship, the family, and friendship, generated weak rights to privacy. In 4th-century BCE Athens, on the other hand, privacy rights were accorded stronger protection. His conclusion was that privacy of communication was attainable only in a complex society with strong liberal traditions.

Our modern demarcation of public and private zones occurred as a result of a twin movement in political and legal thought. The emergence of the nation-state and theories of sovereignty in the 16th and 17th centuries generated the concept of a distinctly public realm. On the other hand, the identification of a private domain free from the encroachment of the state emerged as a response to the claims of monarchs, and, in due course, parliaments, to an untrammelled power to make law. In other words, the appearance of the modern state, the regulation of social and economic activities, and the recognition of a private realm, are natural prerequisites to this separation.

Historical evidence, however, tells only part of the story. Sociological models powerfully express the social values that capture this transformation. A particularly useful sociological dichotomy is the distinction between *Gemeinschaft* and *Gesellschaft*. The former, broadly speaking, is a community of internalized norms and traditions regulated according to status but mediated by love, duty, and a shared understanding and purpose. *Gesellschaft*, on the other hand, is a society in which self-interested individuals compete for personal material advantage in a so-called free market.

This distinction is often expressed as the difference between community and association. The former exhibits almost no division between the public and the private, while in the latter the separation is stark: the law formally regulates that which is conceived to be public. This differentiation illuminates also the political and economic order.

The segregation of public and private spheres is also a central tenet of liberalism. Indeed, 'liberalism may be said largely to have been an argument about where the boundaries of [the] private sphere lie, according to what principles they are to be drawn, whence interference derives and how it is to be checked'. The extent to which the law might legitimately intrude upon the 'private' is a recurring theme, especially in 19th-century liberal doctrine: 'One of the central goals of nineteenth-century legal thought was to create a clear separation between constitutional, criminal, and regulatory law—public law—and the law of private transactions— torts, contracts, property, and commercial law.' And the question of the limits of the criminal law in enforcing 'private morality' continues to perplex legal and moral philosophers.

More than 150 years since its publication, John Stuart Mill's 'harm principle', expounded in *On Liberty*, still provides a litmus test for most libertarian accounts of the limits of interference in the private lives of individuals. For Mill:

> the sole end for which mankind are warranted, individually or collectively in interfering with the liberty of action of any of their number, is self-protection. That the only purpose for which power can be rightfully exercised over any member of a civilized community, against his will, is to prevent harm to others. His own good, either physical or moral, is not a sufficient warrant.

## The value of privacy

A life without privacy is inconceivable. But what purposes does privacy actually serve? In addition to its significance in liberal democratic theory, privacy stakes out a sphere for creativity, psychological wellbeing, our ability to love, forge social relationships, promote trust, intimacy, and friendship.

In his classic work, Alan Westin identifies four functions of privacy that combine the concept's individual and social dimensions. First, it engenders personal autonomy; the democratic principle of individuality is associated with the need for such autonomy – the desire to avoid manipulation or domination by others. Second, it provides the opportunity for emotional release. Privacy allows us to remove our social mask:

On any given day a man may move through the roles of stern father, loving husband, car-pool comedian, skilled lathe operator, union steward, water-cooler flirt, and American Legion committee chairman – all psychologically different roles that he adopts as he moves from scene to scene on the individual stage . . . Privacy . . . gives individuals, from factory workers to Presidents, a chance to lay their masks aside for rest. To be always 'on' would destroy the human organism.

Third, it allows us to engage in self-evaluation – the ability to formulate and test creative and moral activities and ideas. And, fourth, privacy offers us the environment in which we can share confidences and intimacies, and engage in limited and protected communication.

### Private peccadilloes

The backstage language consists of reciprocal first-naming, co-operative decision-making, profanity, open sexual remarks, elaborate griping, smoking, rough informal dress, 'sloppy' sitting and standing posture, use of dialect or sub-standard speech, mumbling and shouting, playful aggression and 'kidding', inconsiderateness for the other in minor but potentially symbolic acts, minor physical self-involvements such as humming, whistling, chewing, nibbling, belching and flatulence.

Erving Goffman, *The Presentation of Self in Everyday Life* (Doubleday Anchor, 1959), p. 128

## The dilemma of privacy

Yet privacy is not an unqualified good. Seven shortcomings may briefly be identified. First, privacy is sometimes perceived as a rather quaint, prudish Victorian value; it has, in the words of one writer, 'an air of injured gentility'. Second, and more seriously, the shroud of privacy may conceal domestic oppression, especially of

## Privacy and female oppression

[W]hen the law of privacy restricts intrusions into intimacy, it bars change in control over that intimacy... It is probably not coincidence that the very things feminism regards as central to the subjection of women – the very place, the body; the very relations, heterosexual; the very activities, intercourse and reproduction; and the very feelings, intimate – form the core of what is covered by privacy doctrine. From this perspective, the legal concept of privacy can and has shielded the place of battery, marital rape, and women's exploited labor.

Catharine MacKinnon, *Feminism Unmodified: Discourses on Life and Law* (Harvard University Press, 1987), p. 101

women by men. Feminists claim that a significant cause of women's subjugation is their relegation to the private realm of the home and family. Moreover, while the state is disposed to control the public sphere, there is a reluctance to encroach into the private realm – frequently the site of the exploitation of and violence against women.

Third, the sanctuary of privacy may weaken the detection and apprehension of criminals and terrorists. Today, of course, threats to security occupy centre-stage. Some fear that an excessively zealous defence of privacy may hinder law-enforcement authorities in the execution of their responsibilities. Fourth, it may hamper the free flow of information, impeding transparency and candour. Fifth, privacy may obstruct business efficiency and increase costs. An undue preoccupation with privacy can undermine the collection of crucial personal information, and slow down the making of commercial decisions, thereby reducing productivity.

Sixth, certain communitarian critics regard privacy as an unduly individualistic right that should not be permitted to trump other rights or community values. Finally, a powerful case is made against privacy by those, like the American judge and jurist Richard Posner, who argue – from an economic standpoint – that withholding unflattering personal information may constitute a form of deception. This important critique warrants closer examination.

In seeking to withhold or limit the circulation of personal information, is the individual engaged in a form of deception, especially when the information depicts him in an unfavourable light? Posner asserts:

> To the extent that people conceal personal information in order to mislead, the economic case for according legal protection to such information is no better than that for permitting fraud in the sale of goods.

But even if one were to recognize the economic perspective, it does not follow that one would accept the assessment of the economic value of withholding personal information. Individuals may be willing to trade their interest in restricting the circulation of such information against their societal interest in its free flow. In other words, Posner has not shown, and may be unable to show, that his calculation of 'competing' interests is necessarily the correct, or even the most likely, one.

Posner also argues that transaction-cost considerations may militate against the legal protection of personal information. Where the information is discrediting and accurate, there is a social incentive to make it generally available: accurate information facilitates reliance on the individual to whom the information relates. It is therefore socially efficient to allow a society a right of access to such information rather than to permit the individual to conceal it. In the case of non-discrediting or false information, the value to the individual of concealment exceeds the value of access to it by the community. Information which is false does not advance rational decision-making and is therefore of little use.

## The meaning of privacy

So far, I have employed the term 'privacy' promiscuously. I have used it to describe a variety of conditions or interests – from seeking refuge to the intimacy of close relations. It is hardly surprising that the notion is anything but coherent. While there is general consensus that our privacy is violated by onslaughts on the private domain – in the shape of surveillance, the interception of our communications, and the activities of the paparazzi, the waters grow ever murkier when a multitude of additional grievances are crowded under the privacy umbrella.

The gargantuan literature on the subject has not produced a lucid or consistent meaning of a value that provides a forum for contesting, amongst other things, the rights of women (especially

8. **The appetite for celebrity gossip fuels an increasingly sensationalist media**

in respect of abortion), the use of contraceptives, the freedom of homosexuals and lesbians, the right to read or view obscene material or pornography, and some of the problems of confidentiality generated by HIV/AIDS. Harnessing privacy in the pursuit of so many disparate, sometimes competing, political ideals has generated a good deal of analytical confusion.

## Privacy apathy

Surveillance technology and the business of daily spying go on largely unnoticed. People have long since gotten used to video cameras, discount cards, and advertising messages ... Although it occasionally annoys him, the transparent citizen appreciates how much easier life is in the computer age. He unhesitatingly forgoes being unobserved, anonymous, unavailable. He has no sense of having less personal freedom. He does not even see that there is something to be defended. He attaches too little importance to his private sphere to want to protect it at the expense of other advantages. Privacy is not a political program that can win votes ... People leave more traces behind than they realize. No longer is one allowed to withdraw from society and live without being pestered ... The individual cannot secretly change masks and become someone else. He can neither disguise himself nor temporarily disappear. His body is regularly X-rayed, his journey through life recorded, and his life changes documented ... Nothing is overlooked, ignored, thrown away ... When every careless act, every error, every fleeting trifle is recorded, there can no longer be any spontaneous action. Everything one does is evaluated and judged. Nothing escapes surveillance. The past suffocates the present ... If data were not erased at regular intervals, people would be imprisoned in the dungeons of their own history. However, this outlook seems to frighten hardly anyone.

Wolfgang Sofsky, *Privacy: A Manifesto* (Princeton University Press, 2008), pp. 7–8

The value of privacy as a general moral, political, or social value is undeniable, but the more the notion is stretched, the greater its ambiguity. In pursuit of clarity, it is arguable that at its heart lies a desire, probably a need, to prevent information about us being known to others without our consent. But, as mentioned above, there are other issues that have increasingly entered the privacy arena. This is most conspicuous in the United States. The expression by the Supreme Court of 'unenumerated rights' such as privacy since its seminal decisions in *Griswold v Connecticut* and *Roe v Wade* (which supported a constitutional right of privacy in respect of contraception and abortion, respectively) has resulted in privacy being equated with the liberty of personal choice: the freedom to pursue various activities, albeit normally in a private place. In other words, the concept of privacy includes the right to control access to and use of bodies. Moreover, since laws regulating abortion and certain sex acts profoundly affect both individual privacy and government power, it may be useful to recognize the category as incorporating the capacity to make personal decisions, what is called 'decisional privacy'.

Incursions into the home, office, or 'private space' have also spawned the idea of 'locational privacy' – an inelegant phrase that captures that feature of privacy invaded by assaults – overt or covert – on the personal domain.

## A definition?

An acceptable definition of privacy remains elusive. Westin's ubiquitous and influential idea conceives of privacy as a claim: the 'claim of individuals, groups, or institutions to determine for themselves when, how, and to what extent information about them is communicated to others'. To regard privacy as a claim (or, the more so, as a right) not only presumes the value of privacy, but fails to define its content. It would, moreover, include the use or disclosure of *any* information about an individual. A similar criticism may be levelled at those conceptions of privacy as an 'area of life' or a psychological state.

Westin's definition has, however, exerted even greater influence in respect of its description of privacy in terms of the extent to which an individual has *control* over information about himself or herself. For control over information to be equated with privacy, an individual would have to be said to have *lost* privacy if he or she is prevented from exercising this control, even if he or she is unable to disclose personal information. This means that the value of privacy is presumed.

Similarly, if I knowingly and voluntarily disclose personal information, I do not thereby lose privacy because I am exercising – rather than relinquishing – control. But this sense of control does not adequately describe privacy, for although I may have control over whether to disclose the information, it may be obtained by other means. And if control is meant in a stronger sense (namely that to disclose information, even voluntarily, constitutes a loss of control because I am no longer able to curtail the dissemination of the information by others), it describes the *potential* rather than the *actual* loss of privacy.

Consequently, I may not attract any interest from others and therefore my privacy will receive protection whether or not I desire it! There is a distinction between my controlling the flow of information about myself, and my being known about in fact. In order to establish whether such control actually protects my privacy, according to this argument, it is also necessary to know, for instance, whether the recipient of the information is bound by restrictive norms.

Furthermore, if privacy is regarded as an aspect of broad-spectrum control (or autonomy), it is assumed that what is at issue is my freedom to choose privacy. But, as suggested above, you may choose to abandon your privacy; the control-based definition therefore relates to the question of which choices you exercise rather than the manner in which you exercise them. It is, in other words, a definition which presupposes the value of privacy.

In view of these headaches, may the answer lie in attempting to describe the characteristics of privacy? Again, however, considerable disagreement exists. One view is that privacy consists of 'limited accessibility' – a cluster of three related but independent components: *secrecy*: information known about an individual; *anonymity*: attention paid to an individual; and *solitude*: physical access to an individual.

A loss of privacy, as distinct from an infringement of a right of privacy, occurs, in this account, where others obtain information about an individual, pay attention, or gain access to him or her. The claimed virtues of this approach are, first, that it is neutral, facilitating an objective identification of a loss of privacy. Second, it demonstrates the coherence of privacy as a value. Third, it suggests the utility of the concept in legal contexts (for it identifies those occasions calling for legal protection). And fourth, it includes 'typical' invasions of privacy and excludes those issues mentioned above which, though often thought to be privacy questions, are best regarded as moral or legal issues in their own right (noise, odours, prohibition of abortion, contraception, homosexuality, and so on).

Yet even this analysis presents difficulties. In particular, to avoid presuming the value of privacy, the analysis rejects definitions that limit themselves to the *quality* of the information divulged. It therefore dismisses the view that, to constitute a part of privacy, the information concerned must be 'private' in the sense of being intimate or related to the individual's identity. If a loss of privacy occurs whenever *any* information about an individual becomes known (the secrecy component), the concept is severely diluted.

It is a distortion to describe *every* instance of the dissemination of information about an individual as a loss of privacy. To the extent, however, that privacy is a function of information or knowledge about the individual, this seems to be inescapable. In other words, in so far as the question of information about an individual is concerned, some limiting or controlling factor is required. The most acceptable factor is arguably that the information be 'personal'.

To claim that whenever an individual is the subject of attention or when access to him is gained he or she necessarily loses privacy is again to divest our concern for privacy of much of its meaning. Having attention focused upon you or being subjected to uninvited intrusions upon your solitude are objectionable in their own right, but our concern for the individual's privacy in these circumstances is strongest when he or she is engaged in activities which we would normally consider private. The Peeping Tom is more likely to affront our conception of what is 'private' than someone who follows us in public.

It is sometimes argued that by protecting the values underpinning privacy (property rights, human dignity, preventing or compensating the infliction of emotional distress, and so on), moral and legal discourse concerning privacy may be dispensed with. If true, this would undercut the conceptual distinctiveness of privacy. Second, even among those who deny the derivative character of privacy, there is little agreement concerning its principal defining features.

Worse, arguments about the meaning of privacy frequently proceed from fundamentally different premises. Thus, where it is described as a 'right', the issue is not seriously joined with those who regard it as a 'condition'. The former is usually a normative statement about the need for privacy (however defined); the latter merely makes a descriptive statement about 'privacy'. Moreover, claims about the desirability of privacy tend to confuse its instrumental and inherent value; privacy is regarded by some as an end in itself, while others view it as a means by which to

secure other social ends such as creativity, love, or
emotional release.

## Privacy and personal information

Is there another way? Without undermining the significance of
privacy as an essential value, could the answer lie in isolating the
issues that give rise to individuals' claims? There is little doubt that
originally the archetypal complaints in the privacy field related to
what the American law calls 'public disclosure of private facts' and
'intrusion upon an individual's seclusion, solitude or private
affairs'. More recently, the collection and use of computerized
personal data, and other issues associated with our electronic
society, have, of course, become major privacy concerns.

It seems clear that, at bottom, these questions share a concern to
limit the extent to which private facts about the individual are
respectively published, intruded upon, or misused. This is not to
suggest that certain conditions (for instance, being alone) or
certain activities (such as telephone-tapping) ought not to be
characterized as privacy or invasions of privacy respectively.

In locating the problems of privacy at the level of personal
information, two obvious questions arise. First, what is to be
understood by 'personal' and, second, under what circumstances is
a matter to be regarded as 'personal'? Is something 'personal' by
virtue simply of the claim by an individual that it is so, or are there
matters that are *intrinsically* personal? To claim that my political
views are personal must depend on certain norms which prohibit
or curtail inquiries into, or unauthorized reports of, such views. It
may, however, suffice for me to invoke the norm that I am entitled
to keep my views to myself.

These norms are clearly culture-relative as well as variable. As
mentioned above, anthropological evidence suggests that primitive

## Buying and selling privacy

You do not strike a deal about personal or private information. The law does not offer you a monopoly right in exchange for your publication of these facts. That is what is distinct about privacy: individuals should be able to control information about themselves. We should be eager to help them protect that information by giving them the structures and the rights to do so. We value, or want, our peace. And thus, a regime that allows us such peace by giving us control over private information is a regime consonant with public values. It is a regime that public authorities should support ... (N)othing in my regime would give individuals final or complete control over the kinds of data they can sell, or the kinds of privacy they can buy. The P3P regime would in principle enable upstream control of privacy rights as well as individual control ... (T)here is no reason such a regime would have to protect all kinds of private data ... there may be facts about yourself that you are not permitted to hide; more important, there may be claims about yourself that you are not permitted to make ('I am a lawyer', or 'Call me, I am a doctor'). You should not be permitted to engage in fraud or to do harm to others.

Lawrence Lessig, *Code and Other Laws of Cyberspace* (Basic Books, 1999), pp. 162–3

societies have differential privacy attitudes. And it can hardly be doubted that in modern societies, conceptions of what is 'private' will fluctuate. There is certainly less diffidence in most modern communities with regard to several aspects of private life than characterized societies of even 50 years ago. Is there not a class of information that may plausibly be described as 'personal'? Normally it is objected that 'privateness' is not an attribute of the information itself; that the *same* information may be regarded as very private in one context and not so private or not private at all in another.

## Anti-privacy moments

The last decade seems to have generated more than its share of what one might call 'anti-privacy moments' – moods in public opinion characterized by willingness to let more and more personal data slip out of individual control. The shock of mass terrorism in Europe and North America has been one impetus to such moods, though hardly the only one. What the last ten years do not seem to have yielded is more moments like Watergate or the revolt against excessive census demands in Germany – dramas that sharpen the public's immune reactions against privacy invasion, and consolidate the institutions and practices built upon such reaction.

James B. Rule, in J. B. Rule and G. Greenleaf (eds.), *Global Privacy Protection: The First Generation* (Edward Elgar, 2008), pp. 272–3

Naturally, Jane may be more inclined to divulge intimate facts to her analyst or to a close friend than to her employer or partner. And her objection to the disclosure of the information by a newspaper might be expected to be even stronger. But the information remains 'personal' in all three contexts. What changes is the extent to which she is prepared to permit the information to become known or to be used. It is counter-intuitive to describe the information in the first context (the analyst) as 'not private at all' or even 'not so private'. We should surely want to say that the psychiatrist is listening to *personal* facts being discussed. Were the conversation to be surreptitiously recorded or the psychiatrist called upon to testify in court as to his patient's homosexuality or infidelity, we should want to say that *personal information* was being recorded or disclosed. The context has manifestly changed, but it affects the degree to which it would be reasonable to expect the individual to object to the information being used or spread abroad, not the *quality* of the information itself.

Any definition of 'personal information' must therefore include both elements. It should refer both to the *quality* of the information and to the *reasonable expectations of the individual concerning its use.* The one is, in large measure, a function of the other. In other words, the concept of 'personal information' postulated here is both descriptive and normative.

Personal information includes those facts, communications, or opinions which relate to the individual and which it would be reasonable to expect him or her to regard as intimate or sensitive, and therefore to want to withhold, or at least to restrict their collection, use, or circulation. 'Facts' are not, of course, confined to textual data, but encompass a wide range of information, including images, DNA, and other genetic and biometric data such as fingerprints, face and iris recognition, and the ever-increasing types of information about us that technology is able to uncover and exploit.

## Greater clarity?

It might immediately be objected that, by resting the notion of 'personal information' on an *objective* determination of an individual's expectations, the definition is actually an exclusively normative one and therefore pre-empts enquiries concerning the desirability or otherwise of protecting 'personal information'. But any attempt to classify information as 'personal', 'sensitive', or 'intimate' entails an assumption that such information warrants special treatment.

To the extent that it is necessary to define the information by reference to some objective criterion, it is inevitable that the classification depends on what may legitimately be claimed to be 'personal'. Only information which it is reasonable to wish to withhold is likely, under any test, to be the focus of our concern, particularly if we are seeking its effective legal protection. An individual who regards information concerning, say, his automobile, as personal and therefore seeks to withhold details of the size of its engine will find it difficult to persuade anyone that his vehicle's registration document constitutes a disclosure of 'personal information'. An objective test of what is 'personal' will normally operate to exclude such species of information.

But this becomes more difficult where the individual's claim relates to information that affects her private life. It would not be unreasonable, for instance, for an individual to wish to prevent the disclosure of facts concerning her trial and conviction for theft. Applying the proposed definition of personal information as a first-order test of whether such information is personal may suggest that the claim is a legitimate one. But it is likely to be defeated on the ground that the administration of justice is an open and public process. The passage of time may, however, alter the nature of such events and what was once a *public* matter may, several years later, be reasonably considered as private.

Similarly, the publication of what was once public information garnered from old newspapers may several years later be considered an offensive disclosure of personal information. It does not therefore follow that the objective test pre-empts the balancing of the individual's right or claim to withhold personal information, on the one hand, against the competing interests of the community in, say, freedom of expression, on the other. By voluntarily disclosing or acceding to the use or dissemination of personal information, the individual does not relinquish his or her claim that he or she retains certain control over it. He or she may, for instance, allow the information to be used for one purpose (such as medical diagnosis), but object when it is used for another (such as employment).

With regard to opinions about an individual expressed by a third party, the existence of which the individual is *aware* (such as references sought for a job application), it would be reasonable to expect her to permit access to such material only by those who are directly concerned in the decision whether or not to employ her. Where she does *not* know that assessments have been made about her (where, for example, she is described as a 'bad risk' on the database of a credit reference agency) or that her communications have been intercepted or recorded, she may reasonably be expected to object to the use or disclosure (and in the case of surreptitious surveillance, to the actual acquisition) of the information, particularly if it is – actually or potentially – misleading or inaccurate *were she aware* of its existence.

It is true that on its own, an item of information may be perfectly innocuous, but when combined with another piece of equally inoffensive data, the information is transformed into something that is genuinely private. So Ms Wong's address is publicly available and, on its own, hardly constitutes 'private' information. Connect this with, say, her occupation, and the combination converts the data into vulnerable details that she has a legitimate interest in concealing.

An objective notion of personal information does not neglect the need to consider the complete context in which the data occur. In evaluating whether the information in question satisfies the threshold requirement of 'personal', the facts that are the subject of the individual's complaint will plainly need to be examined 'in the round'. It is hardly reasonable for victims to conceive of publicly accessible data (telephone numbers, addresses, number plates, etc.) as information whose disclosure or circulation they wish to control or curtail. In general, it is only when these data are rendered sensitive, for example by their linkage to other data, that a justifiable complaint could be said to materialize.

Reasonableness does not wholly exclude the operation of individual idiosyncrasy where its effect would be relevant to the circumstances of the case. Nor would an objective test deny the significance of such factors in determining whether it is reasonable for an individual to consider information as personal. The British, for example, are notoriously coy about revealing their salaries: Scandinavians far less so. Cultural factors will inevitably influence the judgement of whether it is reasonable to regard information as personal. And this is no less true within a specific society.

In any event, no item of information is – in and of itself – personal. An anonymous medical file, bank statement, or lurid disclosure of a sexual affair is innocuous until linked to an individual. Only when the identity of the subject of the information is revealed does it become personal. And this is no less true once this threshold is crossed; what is now personal information is worthy of protection only when it satisfies an objective test. But this does not occur in a conceptual or social vacuum; it must be evaluated by reference to the specific conditions.

Despite disagreement over the meaning, scope, and limits of privacy, there is little uncertainty about its significance and the threats to its preservation. Few doubt that the erosion of this fundamental value must be checked. The next chapter considers its recognition as a legal right.

# Chapter 3
# A legal right

Queen Victoria and Prince Albert were accomplished etchers. In 1849, the royal couple wanted copies made for their private use, and sent a number of plates of their etchings to the palace printer, one Strange. Several of the impressions somehow fell into the hands of a third party, Judge, who evidently obtained them through a 'mole' employed by Strange. In turn, Strange acquired them from Judge in the honest belief that they were to be publicly exhibited with the consent of Victoria and Albert. A catalogue was produced and they set about arranging the exhibition. When he learned that royal assent was nonexistent, Strange withdrew his participation from the exhibition, but decided to proceed with the printing of the catalogue. His proposal was to offer it for sale along with autographs of their regal artists.

The royal couple was not amused. The prince sought an injunction to prevent the exhibition and the intended circulation of the catalogue. It was, needless to say, granted, the court shamelessly acknowledging that 'the importance which has been attached to this case arises entirely from the exalted station of the Plaintiff . . .'.

Though the judgments in the case turn largely on the fact that the plates were the property of the prince, the court explicitly

9. The royal couple was not amused

recognized that this afforded a wider basis upon which the law 'shelters the privacy and seclusion of thoughts and sentiments committed to writing, and desired by the author to remain not generally known'.

# The American genesis

This decision was a significant factor in the legendary article that in 1890 was to give birth to the legal recognition of privacy in its own right. Written by Samuel D. Warren and Louis D. Brandeis, their commentary was published in the influential *Harvard Law Review*. A few years before, the invention of the inexpensive and portable 'snap camera' by Eastman Kodak had changed the world. Individuals could be snapped at home, at work, or at play. The beginning of the end of privacy was nigh.

The two lawyers, Warren, a Boston attorney and socialite, and Brandeis, who would be appointed to the Supreme Court in 1916, angered by nascent media intrusion, so-called 'yellow journalism', wrote what is widely characterized as the most influential law review article ever published. It is often thought that the catalyst for their anger was that the press had snooped on Warren's daughter's wedding. But this seems unlikely since, in 1890, she was six years old! The more likely source of their irritation was a series of articles in a Boston high-society gossip magazine, describing Warren's swanky dinner parties.

In any event, the celebrated article condemned the press for their effrontery (foreshadowing also the threat to privacy posed by Kodak's new-fangled contraption), and contended that the common law implicitly recognized the right to privacy. Drawing upon decisions of the English courts relating to, in particular, breach of confidence, property, copyright, and defamation, they argued that these cases were merely instances and applications of a general right to privacy. The common law, they claimed, albeit under different forms, protected an individual whose privacy was invaded by the likes of a snooping journalist. In so doing, the law acknowledged the importance of the spiritual and intellectual needs of man. They famously declared:

10. The seminal 1890 article by Samuel Warren and his partner
Louis Brandeis (above), who was later to become a distinguished
member of the United States Supreme Court, expounded the claim
that the common law protected the right of privacy

The intensity and complexity of life, attendant upon advancing civilization, have rendered necessary some retreat from the world, and man, under the refining influence of culture, has become more sensitive to publicity so that solitude and privacy have become more essential to the individual; but modern enterprise and invention have, through invasion upon his privacy, subjected him to mental pain and distress, far greater than could be inflicted by mere bodily injury.

The common law, they reasoned, has developed from the protection of the physical person and corporeal property to the protection of the individual's '[t]houghts, emotions and sensations'. But as a result of threats to privacy from recent inventions and business methods and from the press, the common law needed to go further. An individual's right to determine the extent to which his thoughts, emotions, and sensations were communicated to others was already legally protected but only in respect of authors of literary and artistic compositions and letters who could forbid their unauthorized publication. And though English cases recognizing this right were based on protection of property, in reality they were an acknowledgement of privacy, of 'inviolate personality'.

It was not long before their line of reasoning was put to the test. In 1902, the plaintiff complained that her image had been used without her consent to advertise the defendant's merchandise. She was portrayed on bags of flour with the dismal pun, 'Flour of the family'. The majority of the New York Court of Appeals rejected Warren and Brandeis's thesis, holding that the privacy argument had 'not as yet an abiding place in our jurisprudence, and . . . cannot now be incorporated without doing violence to settled principles of law . . .'. The minority, however, warmed to the idea, Gray J declaring that the plaintiff had a right to be protected against the use of her image for the defendant's commercial advantage: 'Any other principle of decision . . . is as repugnant to equity as it is shocking to reason.'

## The iniquity of gossip

Gossip is no longer the resource of the idle and of the vicious, but has become a trade, which is pursued with industry as well as effrontery. To satisfy a prurient taste the details of sexual relations are spread broadcast in the columns of the daily papers. To occupy the indolent, column upon column is filled with idle gossip, which can only be procured by intrusion upon the domestic circle ... Nor is the harm wrought by such invasions confined to the suffering of those who may be the subjects of journalistic or other enterprise. In this, as in other branches of commerce, the supply creates the demand. Each crop of unseemly gossip, thus harvested, becomes the seed of more, and, in direct proportion to its circulation, results in the lowering of social standards and of morality. Even gossip apparently harmless, when widely and persistently circulated, is potent for evil. It both belittles and perverts. It belittles by inverting the relative importance of things, thus dwarfing the thoughts and aspirations of a people. When personal gossip attains the dignity of print, and crowds the space available for matters of real interest to the community, what wonder that the ignorant and thoughtless mistake its relative importance. Easy of comprehension, appealing to that weak side of human nature which is never wholly cast down by the misfortunes and frailties of our neighbors, no one can be surprised that it usurps the place of interest in brains capable of other things. Triviality destroys at once robustness of thought and delicacy of feeling. No enthusiasm can flourish, no generous impulse can survive under its blighting influence.

Samuel D. Warren and Louis D. Brandeis, 'The Right to Privacy' (1890) 5 *Harvard Law Review* 196

The court's decision provoked general discontent. This led to the enactment by the State of New York of a statute that rendered the unauthorized use of an individual's name or image for advertising or trade purposes unlawful. But three years later, in a case involving similar facts, the Supreme Court of Georgia adopted the reasoning of Gray J. The Warren and Brandeis argument, 15 years after its publication, had prevailed. Most American states have since incorporated the 'right to privacy' into their law. Yet, despite the authors' heavy reliance on the judgments of English courts, no comparable development has occurred in England or in other common law jurisdictions.

Over the years, the American common law maintained its steady expansion of the protection of privacy. In 1960, Dean Prosser, a leading tort expert, expounded the view that the law now recognized not one tort, 'but a complex of four different interests ... tied together by the common name, but otherwise [with] nothing in common'. He delineated their nature as follows:

> The first tort consists in intruding upon the plaintiff's seclusion or solitude or into his private affairs. The wrongful act is the intentional interference with the plaintiff's solitude or seclusion. It includes the physical intrusion into the plaintiff's premises and eavesdropping (including electronic and photographic surveillance, bugging, and telephone-tapping). Three requirements must be satisfied: (a) there must be an actual prying; (b) the intrusion must offend a reasonable man; (c) it must be an intrusion into something private.

The second tort is the public disclosure of embarrassing private facts about the plaintiff. Prosser distinguished three elements of the tort:

> (a) there must be publicity (to disclose the facts to a small group of people would not suffice); (b) the facts disclosed must be private facts (publicity given to matters of public record is not tortious); (c) the facts disclosed must be offensive to a reasonable man of ordinary sensibilities.

Third, he identified a tort that consists of publicity that places the plaintiff in a false light in the public eye. This is usually committed where an opinion or utterance (such as spurious books or views) is publicly attributed to the plaintiff or where his picture is used to illustrate a book or article with which he has no reasonable connection. The publicity must again be 'highly offensive to a reasonable person'.

Finally, Prosser distinguished the tort of appropriation, for the defendant's advantage, of the plaintiff's name or likeness. The advantage derived by the defendant need not be a financial one; it has, for instance, been held to arise where the plaintiff was wrongly named as father on a birth certificate. The statutory tort, which exists in several states, on the other hand, normally requires the unauthorized use of the plaintiff's identity for commercial (usually advertising) purposes. The recognition of this tort establishes what has been dubbed a 'right of publicity' under which an individual is able to decide how he or she desires to exploit his or her name or image commercially. The four forms of invasion of privacy, according to Prosser, were connected only in that each constituted an interference with the 'right to be let alone'.

This fourfold segregation of the right to privacy is regarded by some as misconceived because it undermines the Warren and Brandeis axiom of 'inviolate personality' and neglects its moral basis as an aspect of human dignity. The classification has nevertheless assumed a prominent place in American tort law, although, as predicted by one legal scholar, Harry Kalven, it has to a large extent ossified the conception into four types:

> [G]iven the legal mind's weakness for neat labels and categories and given the deserved Prosser prestige, it is a safe prediction that the fourfold view will come to dominate whatever thinking is done about the right of privacy in the future.

The vicissitudes of these four torts have been charted in an immense torrent of academic and popular literature. Nor has this development been restricted to the United States. Virtually every advanced legal system has, to a greater or lesser extent, sought to recognize certain aspects of privacy. These include Austria, Canada, China and Taiwan, Denmark, Estonia, France, Germany, Holland, Hungary, Ireland, India, Italy, Lithuania, New Zealand, Norway, the Philippines, Russia, South Africa, South Korea, Spain, Thailand, and the majority of Latin American countries.

## A constitutional right

These four torts remained the effective means by which the American law protected privacy. And they marked, more or less, the confines of the constitutional protection of privacy as well. The principal concern of Warren and Brandeis was, of course, what we would now call media intrusion. Several years later, however, Justice Brandeis (as he now was) delivered a powerful dissent in the case of *Olmstead v United States* in 1928. He declared that the Constitution conferred 'as against the Government, the right to be let alone', adding, 'To protect that right, every unjustifiable intrusion by the Government upon the privacy of the individual, whatever the means employed, must be deemed a violation of the Fourth Amendment.' That view was adopted by the Supreme Court in *Katz v United States*. Since then privacy as the right to be let alone has repeatedly been invoked by the Supreme Court.

The most significant – and controversial – development came in 1965 with the Supreme Court's decision in *Griswold v Connecticut*. It declared unconstitutional a Connecticut statute prohibiting the use of contraceptives – because it violated the right of marital privacy, a right 'older than the Bill of Rights'. The Constitution makes no mention of the right of privacy. Yet in a series of cases the Supreme Court has – via the Bill of Rights (particularly the First, Third, Fourth, Fifth, and Ninth Amendments) – recognized, amongst other privacy rights, that of 'associational privacy', 'political privacy', and 'privacy of counsel'. It has also set the limits of protection against eavesdropping and unlawful searches.

By far the most divisive 'privacy' decision that the Court has decided is the case of *Roe v Wade* in 1973. It held, by a majority, that the abortion law of Texas was unconstitutional as a violation of the right to privacy. Under that law, abortion was criminalized, except when performed to save the pregnant woman's life. The Court held that states may prohibit abortion to protect the life of the foetus only in the third trimester. The judgment, which has been described as 'undoubtedly the best-known case the United States Supreme Court has ever decided', is concurrently welcomed by feminists, and deplored by many Christians. It is the slender thread by which the right of American women to a lawful abortion hangs. There appears to be no middle ground. The jurist Ronald Dworkin forthrightly depicts the intensity of the skirmish:

> The war between anti-abortion groups and their opponents is America's new version of the terrible seventeenth-century European civil wars of religion. Opposing armies march down streets or pack themselves into protests at abortion clinics, courthouses, and the White House, screaming at and spitting on and loathing one another. Abortion is tearing America apart.

Another 'privacy' judgment of the Court that generated a hullabaloo was *Bowers v Hardwick* in 1986, in which a bare majority held that the privacy protections of the due process clause did not extend to homosexual acts between consenting adults in private: 'No connection between family, marriage, or procreation on the one hand and homosexual conduct on the other has been demonstrated.'

This decision was explicitly overruled in *Lawrence v Texas* in which, by 6 to 3, the Supreme Court decided that it had construed the liberty interest too narrowly. The majority held that substantive due process under the Fourteenth Amendment entailed the freedom to engage in intimate consensual sexual conduct. Its effect is to nullify all legislation throughout the United

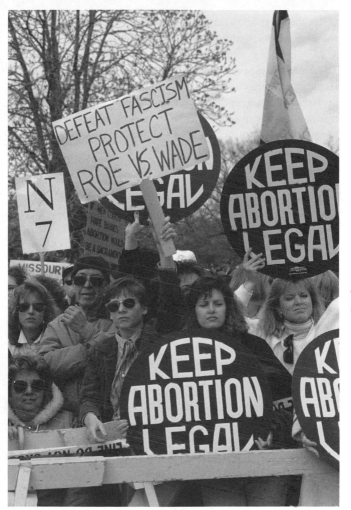

A legal right

11. The United States Supreme Court's decision of *Roe v Wade* in 1973 sparked a controversy that persists to this day

States that purports to criminalize sodomy between consenting same-sex adults in private.

The American experience is both influential and instructive. Other common law jurisdictions continue to wrestle with the intractable problems of definition, scope, and reconciling privacy with other rights, especially freedom of expression. It is fair to say, as a generalization, that the preference of the common law is interest-based, while the continental tradition of civil law jurisdictions tends to be rights-based. In other words, while the English law, for example, adopts a pragmatic case-by-case approach to the protection of privacy, French law conceives of privacy as a fundamental human right. This disparity has nevertheless been attenuated by the impact of the European Convention on Human Rights and other declarations and directives emanating from Brussels. The intensity of this side-wind is most conspicuously

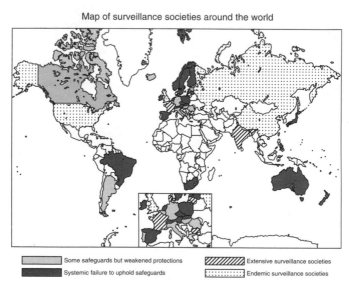

Map of surveillance societies around the world

| | |
|---|---|
| Some safeguards but weakened protections | Extensive surveillance societies |
| Systemic failure to uphold safeguards | Endemic surveillance societies |

12. **Privacy is accorded differential protection across the globe**

evident in the adoption by the United Kingdom in its Human Rights Act of 1998, as will become clear below.

## Common law tribulations

It is not only the law of England and Wales that still grapples with the predicament of privacy. Australia, New Zealand, Ireland, Canada, Hong Kong, and other common law jurisdictions languish in a quagmire of indecision and hesitancy.

The English law, despite several commissions, committees, and attempts at legislation, remains uncertain and ambiguous. In 1972, the Younger Committee rejected the idea of a general right of privacy created by statute. It concluded that it would burden the court 'with controversial questions of a social and political character'. Judges would be likely to encounter problems balancing privacy with competing interests such as freedom of expression. The committee recommended the creation of a new crime and tort of unlawful surveillance, a new tort of disclosure or other use of information unlawfully acquired, and the consideration of the law on breach of confidence (which protects confidential information entrusted by one party to another) as a possible means by which privacy could be safeguarded. Similar reports have been produced in other common law jurisdictions.

In recent years, a spate of celebrity litigation has presented the courts with an opportunity to examine whether, in the absence of explicit common law privacy protection, the remedy of breach of confidence might provide a makeshift solution. These are best considered in Chapter 4. They demonstrate how a right of privacy is slouching towards the highest court to be born. One such case, involved the publication of photographs taken surreptitiously of the wedding of movie stars Michael Douglas and Catherine Zeta-Jones, and is also discussed in Chapter 4. Lord Hoffmann has declared in the House of Lords that the:

coming into force of the Human Rights Act 1998 weakens the argument for saying that a general tort of invasion of privacy is needed to fill gaps in the existing remedies. Sections 6 and 7 of the Act are in themselves substantial gap fillers; if it is indeed the case that a person's rights under Article 8 have been infringed by a public authority, he will have a statutory remedy. The creation of a general tort will.... pre-empt the controversial question of the extent, if any, to which the Convention requires the state to provide remedies for invasions of privacy by persons who are not public authorities.

The impact of this Act (which incorporates into English law Article 8 of the European Convention on Human Rights) cannot be overstated. It provides for the protection of the right to respect for family life, home, and correspondence. This measure, at least in the mind of one senior judge, gives 'the final impetus to the recognition of a right of privacy in English law'. Though his conviction may not be shared by all members of the judiciary, the analysis of privacy exhibited in recent cases suggests that the effect of Article 8 is to supply, at least, the potential for the horizontal application of the rights in this Article. Indeed, it is not unreasonable to identify in a number of recent judgments a willingness to allow Article 8 to thwart the birth of a full-blown privacy tort. One can almost hear the clank of the sword being returned to its scabbard.

As in Britain, deliberations about the need for legal protection have preoccupied law-reform commissions at both state and federal level in Australia. Nor have the courts been idle. In a significant decision in 2001, a majority of the High Court of Australia tilted gingerly towards the recognition of a privacy tort. In *Australian Broadcasting Corporation v Lenah Game Meats Pty Ltd*, the court, acknowledging the inadequacy of Australian law, expressed its support for the judicial development in common law jurisdictions of a common law action for invasion of privacy. In specifying what

13. **Despite attempts to conduct their wedding in private, surreptitious photographs of the Douglases were taken, and became the subject of protracted and significant litigation in England**

might constitute an unwarranted invasion of privacy, the court stated:

> Certain kinds of information about a person, such as information relating to health, personal relationships, or finances, may be easy to identify as private; as may certain kinds of activity, which a reasonable person, applying contemporary standards of morals and behaviour, would understand to be meant to be unobserved. The requirement that disclosure or observation of information or conduct would be highly offensive to a reasonable person of ordinary sensibilities is in many circumstances a useful practical test of what is private.

The decision, though inconclusive on the central issue, does suggest that the High Court, when presented with a more deserving plaintiff (this one was an abattoir whose cruel practices the Australian Broadcasting Corporation wished expose), may recognize that a privacy tort may not be entirely unthinkable.

In 2005, the New Zealand Court of Appeal took a significant step towards recognizing a common law tort of privacy. In the case of *Hosking v Runting*, the defendants took pictures of the plaintiffs' 18-month-old twin daughters in the street, being pushed in their buggy by their mother. The father is a well-known television personality. The couple sought an injunction to prevent publication. The trial court held that New Zealand law did not recognize a cause of action in privacy based on the public disclosure of photographs taken in a public place. But, though the Court of Appeal dismissed the plaintiffs' appeal, it decided (by 3 to 2) that a case had been made out for a remedy for 'breach of privacy by giving publicity to private and personal information'. This view was based principally upon its interpretation of the English courts' analysis of the remedy for breach of confidence, as well as the fact that it was consistent with New Zealand's obligations under the ICCPR and the United Nations Convention on the Rights of the Child. The court also considered that their judgment facilitated the reconciliation of competing values, and enabled New Zealand to draw upon the extensive experience of the United States.

In their judgments, Gault P and Blanchard J specified two essential requirements for a claim to succeed. First, the plaintiff must have a reasonable expectation of privacy; and second, there must be publicity given to private facts that would be considered highly offensive to an objective reasonable person.

The Privacy Act of 1993 provides that any person may complain to the Privacy Commissioner alleging that any action is or appears to be 'an interference with the privacy of an individual'. If the Privacy Commissioner finds that the complaint has substance, he ay refer it to the Proceedings Commissioner appointed under Human Rights Act 1993, who may in turn bring proceedings in the Complaints Review Tribunal. The Tribunal may make an order prohibiting a repetition of the action complained of or requiring the interference to be rectified. It has the power to award damages.

While Ireland does not explicitly recognize a general right to privacy at common law, the courts have fashioned a constitutional right to privacy out of Article 40.3.1 of the Constitution under which the State guarantees to respect, defend, and vindicate the personal rights of the citizen. So, for example, in 1974 the majority of the Supreme Court held that privacy was included among these rights. Succeeding judgments have indicated that the Article extends to some invasions of privacy by interception of communications and surveillance.

## Other approaches

The continental attitude to privacy is based on the concept of the 'right of personality'. In Germany, this right is guaranteed by the Basic Law. Article 1 imposes on all state authorities a duty to respect and protect 'the dignity of man'. Article 2(1) provides that 'Everyone shall have the right to the free development of his personality in so far as he does not violate the rights of others or offend against the constitutional order or the moral code.' These two articles combine to establish a general right to one's own personality; and the right to respect for one's private sphere of life is an emanation of this personality right.

In addition, the courts protect privacy as part of the right of personality under the Civil Code. They also employ the law of delict to provide a remedy against conduct injurious to human dignity such as the unauthorized publication of the intimate details of a person's private life, the right not to publish medical reports without the patient's consent; the right not to have one's conversation recorded without one's knowledge an consent; the right not to have one's private correspondence opened – whether or not it is actually read; the right not to be photographed without consent; the right to a fair description of one's life; and the right not to have personal information misused by the press.

The German courts recognize three spheres of personality: the 'intimate', the 'private', and the 'individual' spheres. The 'intimate sphere' covers one's thoughts and feelings and their expression, medical information, and sexual behaviour. Given its particularly private nature, this species of information enjoys absolute protection. The 'private sphere' includes information which, while neither intimate nor secret (such as facts about one's family and home life), is nevertheless private and therefore attracts qualified protection; disclosure might be justified in the public interest. The 'individual sphere' relates to an individual's public, economic, and professional life, one's social and occupational relations. It attracts the lowest degree of protection.

Privacy is zealously protected in France. Though it is not explicitly mentioned in the French Constitution, the Constitutional Council in 1995 extended the concept of 'individual freedom' in Article 66 to the right to privacy. Privacy was thus elevated to a constitutional right. In addition, Article 9 of the French Civil Code provides that 'Everyone has the right to respect for his private life…'. This has been interpreted by the courts to include a person's identity (name, date of birth, religion, address, and so on) and information about a person's health, matrimonial situation, family, sexual relationships, sexual orientation, and his or her way of life in general. It is also a criminal offence to encroach intentionally upon a private place by taking a photograph or by making a recording. Damages may be awarded for violations.

The Italian Constitution protects the right to privacy as a ɔnstituent of an individual's personality. Thus an invasion of ʋacy may give rise to a claim under the Civil Code, which provides that a person who intentionally or negligently commits an act that causes unreasonable harm to another is liable to compensate the latter. The Civil Code declares also that the publication of a person's image may be restrained if it causes prejudice to his dignity or reputation.

Article 10 of the Dutch Constitution guarantees the right to privacy, but it is a right subject to qualification; though the Supreme Court has held that the right to freedom of speech does not excuse an infringement of privacy, it will consider all circumstances in a privacy action, and a journalist may demonstrate that the publication in question was reasonable. Article 1401 of the Civil Code imposes a general liability for causing wrongful harm to others; it has been interpreted to include harm caused by publishing injurious private information without justification. The criminal law punishes trespassing into a person's home, eavesdropping on private conversations, and the unauthorized taking of photographs of individuals on any private property, and publishing the photograph so acquired.

While neither the Canadian Constitution nor its Charter of Rights and Freedoms include an explicit reference to privacy, the courts have filled the gap by construing the right to be secure against unreasonable search or seizure (Section 8 of the Charter) to embody an individual's right to a reasonable expectation of privacy. There is no common law right of privacy along American lines, but the lower courts have shown a willingness to stretch existing causes of action, such as trespass or nuisance, to protect the privacy of the victim. The common law deficiency has been resolved in a number of Canadian provinces by the enactment of a statutory tort of invasion of privacy. In British Columbia, Manitoba, Newfoundland, and Saskatchewan, the tort of 'violation of privacy' is actionable without proof of damage. The precise formulation the tort differs in each province.

Quebec, as a civil law jurisdiction, has developed its remedy through the interpretation of general provisions of civil liability in the former Civil Code. The present protection, however, is explicitly incorporated in the new Civil Code. It provides that every person has a right to the respect of his reputation and privacy, and that no-one may invade the privacy of another person except with the consent of the person or his heirs, or unless it is authorized by law. The forms of privacy-invading conduct specified cover a fairly wide range of conduct. In addition, Section 5 of the Quebec Charter of Human Rights and Freedoms declares that every person has a right to respect for his private life. This provision is directly enforceable between citizens. The 1994 Uniform Privacy Act clarifies and augments the existing provincial statutes.

## The international dimension

A fairly generous right to privacy is an acknowledged human right, and is recognized in most international instruments. So, for example, Article 12 of the United Nations Declaration of Human Rights and Article 17 of the International Covenant on Civil and Political Rights (ICCPR) both provide:

(1)  No one shall be subjected to arbitrary or unlawful interference with his privacy, family, home or correspondence, nor to unlawful attacks on his honour and reputation.
(2)  Everyone has the right to the protection of the law against such interference or attacks.

Article 8 of the European Convention on Human Rights (ECHR) declares,

(1)  Everyone has the right to respect for his private and family life, his home and his correspondence.

(2) There shall be no interference by a public authority with the exercise of this right except such as is in accordance with the law and is necessary in a democratic society in the interests of national security, public safety or the economic well-being of the country, for the prevention of disorder or crime, for the protection of health or morals, or for the protection of the rights and freedoms of others.

The European Court of Human Rights in Strasbourg has had its hands fairly full adjudicating complaints from individuals seeking redress for alleged infractions of Article 8. Their grievances have exposed deficiencies in the domestic law of several European jurisdictions. For example, in *Gaskin v United Kingdom*, the Court held that the right to respect for private and family life imposed a duty to provide an individual with personal information about himself or herself held by a public authority. In *Leander v Sweden*, the court had ruled that such access could legitimately be denied to an applicant where the information related to national security, for example, for the purpose of vetting an individual for a sensitive position, provided there is a satisfactory process by which the decision not to provide the information may be reviewed. Two of the court's leading decisions in regard to telephone tapping are discussed below.

## Intrusion

Today's spy no longer relies on his unaided eyes and ears. As we saw in Chapter 1, an array of electronic devices renders his task relatively simple. And in the face of these technological advances, the traditional physical or legal means of protection are unlikely to prove particularly effective; the former because radar and laser beams are no respecters of walls or windows; the latter because, in the absence of an encroachment upon the individual's property, the law of trespass will not assist the beleaguered victim of electronic surveillance. The interest protected is the plaintiff's property rather than his privacy.

Physical intrusions into private premises raise similar questions to those generated by the interception of private conversations and correspondence, electronic or otherwise. No civilized society can permit the unauthorized entry and search of a person's home without a valid warrant issued in advance, normally by a court. The prevention, detection, and prosecution of criminal conduct frequently require searches of private premises by the police and other law enforcement authorities. This is a matter that raises deeper questions of policy that extend beyond the protection of privacy. It is nevertheless clear, especially in a modern industrialized society, that electronic surveillance, interception of correspondence, and telephone-tapping call for systematic and fairly elaborate legislative machinery to control, in particular, the circumstances under which the law will permit the use of such devices, and their legitimate application in the pursuit of offenders and the administration of criminal justice.

The laws of many democratic countries regulate the exercise of covert surveillance by a judicial authority. Normally a court order sets out the restrictions, including time limits, on the exercise of this power which is especially pernicious since it involves monitoring not only what the subject says, but also those to whom he or she speaks. Most are likely to be wholly innocent interlocutors.

## Surveillance and terrorism

A powerful weapon in the so-called 'war on terror' is the wiretap. Its use has predictably intensified since the attacks of 11 September 2001. Within six weeks of this date, the United States Congress had enacted the United and Strengthening America by Providing Appropriate Tools Required to Intercept and Obstruct Terrorism

Act (USA PATRIOT Act). This was merely one of several measures that have been introduced to authorize the surveillance of a wide range of activities, including telephone calls, email, and Internet communications, by a number of law-enforcement officials. The provisions of a series of pre-11 September statutes – such as the Wiretap Statute, the Electronic Communications Privacy Act (ECPA), and the Foreign Intelligence Surveillance Act (FISA) – have been substantially amended, significantly diminishing their privacy safeguards.

Privacy advocates and civil libertarians have condemned numerous features of the legislation. Among their concerns is the fact that it reduces the judicial oversight of electronic surveillance by subjecting private Internet communications to a minimal standard of review. The Act also permits law-enforcement authorities to obtain what is, in effect, a 'blank warrant'; it authorizes 'scattershot' intelligence wiretap orders that do not need to specify the place to be searched or require that only the target's conversations be listened to.

Another disquieting feature of the statute is the power it affords the FBI to use its intelligence authority to evade judicial review of the 'probable cause' requirement of the Fourth Amendment which requires that search warrants specify the place to be searched. It prevents abuses such as random searches of the homes of innocent persons based on a warrant obtained to search someone else's home. In other words, in the case of electronic surveillance, the specificity requirement of the Fourth Amendment obliges law-enforcement officers applying for a court order to specify the telephone they wish to tap.

In its celebrated 1967 decision in *Katz v United States*, the Supreme Court held that a listening device placed outside a public telephone booth constituted an unlawful search. The government argued that since the bug was not actually inside the booth, no invasion of the plaintiff's privacy had occurred. Rejecting this vi the Court declared that 'the Fourth Amendment protects people, not places'. Though it has since retreated somewhat from this position, its judgment that protection should turn on whether in the circumstances the individual had a 'reasonable expectation of privacy' remains the hook on which to hang the claim that similar protection ought to apply to communications on the Internet. For the moment, however, the PATRIOT Act, its more recent incarnation, and related measures, place questions such as this on ice.

Prior to its enactment, investigators in terrorism and espionage cases were required to return to the court every time a suspect changed telephones or computers and obtain a fresh warrant.

The Act allows 'roving wiretap' warrants from a secret court to intercept a suspect's phone and Internet conversations, without identifying a specific phone or the suspect. In other words, when the target of a roving wiretap order enters another person's home, law-enforcement agents can tap the homeowner's telephone.

Are these legislative inroads into privacy really necessary? According to the American Civil Liberties Union:

> The FBI already has broad authority to monitor telephone and Internet communications. Current law already provides, for example, that wiretaps can be obtained for the crimes involved in terrorist attacks, including destruction of aircraft and aircraft piracy. Most of the changes to wiretapping authority contemplated in the USA PATRIOT Act would apply not just to surveillance of people suspected of terrorist activity, but to investigation of other crimes as well. The FBI also has authority to intercept communications without probable cause of crime for 'intelligence purposes under the Foreign Intelligence Surveillance Act ('FISA')'. The standards for obtaining a FISA wiretap are lower than those for obtaining a criminal wiretap.

Pen registers and trap-and-trace devices electronically screen telephone or Internet communications. So, a pen register monitors all numbers dialled from a telephone line or all Internet communications are recorded. The PATRIOT Act authorizes a federal judge or magistrate in one area to issue a pen register or a trap-and-trace order that does not specify the name of the Internet Service Provider (ISP) upon which it can be served. Indeed, it can be served on an ISP anywhere in the United States. The judge simply issues the order and law-enforcement agents fill in the locations at which the order can be served, thereby further curtailing the judicial function.

## Modes of approval

Long before the current spate of anti-terrorist measures, the United States had enacted several statutes, both at federal and state level, which set standards to be satisfied before government interception was permitted. Before a warrant is issued under the Electronic Communications Privacy Act 1986 (ECPA), any law-enforcement officer must indicate the nature of the offence under investigation, the interception point, the types of conversations to be intercepted, and the names of the likely targets. He needs to demonstrate probable cause, and that normal investigative techniques are ineffective. Court orders under the Act authorize surveillance for up to 30 days (with the possibility of a 30-day extension). A report must be made to the court every 7 to 10 days.

It is a federal crime to wiretap or to use a machine to capture the communications of others without court approval, unless one of the parties has given their prior consent. It is also a federal offence to use or disclose any information acquired by illegal wiretapping or electronic eavesdropping. Legislation also provides protection against the interception of email and the surreptitious use of telephone-call-monitoring practices. These arrangements include a procedural mechanism to afford limited law-enforcement access to private communications and communications records under conditions consistent with the dictates of the Fourth Amendment that guarantees the right to be free of unreasonable search and seizure, and provides that no warrant shall be issued, save on probable cause.

## A solution?

There is no perfect system. But, at the very least one would expect democratic societies to regulate this highly intrusive form of surveillance in a manner that ensures that the legitimate and reasonable expectations of its citizens are respected. In deciding whether to grant an application for a warrant to carry out covert surveillance, a court ought to satisfy itself that the proposed intrusion has a legitimate purpose. It should ensure that the means of investigation are proportionate to the immediacy and gravity of the alleged offence, balancing the need for the surveillance against the intrusiveness of the activity on the subject and others who may be affected by it. There must be a reasonable suspicion that the target is involved in the commission of a serious crime. It should also be satisfied that information relevant to the purpose of the surveillance is likely to be acquired, and that such information cannot reasonably be obtained by less intrusive means.

In reaching its decision, one would be entitled to assume that a judicial officer would have regard to the immediacy and gravity of the serious crime or the threat to public security, the place where the intrusion will occur, the method of intrusion to be employed, and the nature of any device to be used.

A court should consider the 'reasonable expectation of privacy' in the particular circumstances of the case. In respect of wiretapping, the suggestion is sometimes heard that a telephone user's reasonable expectation of privacy may be vindicated when the eavesdropper turns out to be a private individual, but not when it is the police acting under lawful authority. This is said to be based on the acceptance of risk, but it is difficult to see how such a distinction can be legitimately drawn. If I am entitled to assume that my private conversation will not be overheard by a private individual, why should that assumption be any less strong when the eavesdropper turns out to be the police?

A further recurring difficulty concerns the standards to be applied in the case of 'non-consensual surveillance' as opposed to 'participant monitoring'. The former occurs where a private conversation is intercepted by a person who is not a party to the conversation and who has not obtained the consent of any party to it. 'Participant monitoring' on the other hand, includes cases in which a party uses a listening device to transmit the conversation to one who is not a party, or where a party to the conversation records it without the consent of the other party. It is frequently argued that, while non-consensual surveillance ought to be legally controlled, participant monitoring – especially when used in law enforcement – is justifiable. But this neglects the distinctive interests that underpin the concern to protect the content and, perhaps even more importantly, the manner in which conversations are conducted. Moreover, though participant monitoring is a useful aid in the detection of crime, and arguably constitutes less of a risk to privacy than its non-consensual counterpart, 'the party to the conversation who secretly makes a recording can present matters in a way that is entirely favourable to his position because he controls the situation. He knows he is recording it.'

## Europe

The European Court of Human Rights has been particularly energetic in this area. It is instructive briefly to compare two of its important decisions, one relating to Germany, the other to the

United Kingdom. The telephone-tapping in *Klass v Federal Republic of Germany* complied with the German statute. In *Malone v United Kingdom*, however, it was conducted without a comprehensive legislative framework. Although both involved analogue telephones, the principles expressed are sufficiently general to apply to digital telephony, as well as to the interception of written correspondence, and perhaps also to other forms of surveillance.

German law sets out stringent restrictions on interception including the requirement that applications be made in writing, that a basis exists in fact for suspecting a person of planning, committing, or having committed certain criminal or subversive acts, and that the surveillance may cover only the specific suspect or his presumed contact persons: exploratory or general surveillance is therefore not permitted. The law provides also that it must be shown that other investigatory methods would be ineffective or considerably more difficult. The interception is supervised by a judicial officer who may reveal only information that is relevant to the inquiry; he must destroy the remainder. The intercepted information must itself be destroyed when no longer required, nor may it be used for any other purpose.

The law requires that the interception must be immediately discontinued when these requirements have ended, and the subject must be notified as soon as this is possible without jeopardizing the purpose of the interception. He or she may then challenge the lawfulness of the interception in an administrative court and may claim damages in a civil court if prejudice is proved.

In addition, the German Basic Law protects secrecy of the mail, posts, and telecommunications. The court therefore had to decide whether interference was justified under Article 8(2) of the European Convention as being 'in accordance with the law' and necessary in a democratic society 'in the interests of national security…or for the prevention of disorder or crime'. While the court acknowledged the need for legislation to protect these interests, it held that the question was not the need for such provisions, but whether they contained sufficient safeguards against abuse.

The applicants contended that the legislation violated Article 8 of the European Convention because it lacked a requirement that the subject of the interception be 'invariably' notified following the termination of the surveillance. The Court held that this was not inherently incompatible with Article 8, provided that the subject was informed after the termination of the surveillance measures as soon as notification could be made without endangering the purpose of those measures.

In *Malone v United Kingdom*, the plaintiff, who, at his trial on a number of charges relating to handling stolen property, learned that his telephone conversations had been intercepted, issued a writ against the police. He argued in vain, first, that telephone-tapping was an unlawful infringement of his rights of privacy, property, and confidentiality; second, that it contravened Article 8 of the European Convention on Human Rights; and, third, that the Crown had no legal authority to intercept calls since no such power had been conferred by the law. He took his grievance to the European Court of Human Rights, where, not surprisingly, he succeeded. The Court unanimously held that the Convention had indeed been breached. As a result, the British Government acknowledged that a statute was required, and the Interception of Communications Act of 1985 was enacted. It establishes a fairly comprehensive framework, the centrepiece of which is the provision empowering the Secretary of State to issue warrants where he or she considers it necessary in the interests of national security, to prevent or detect serious crime, or safeguard economic wellbeing.

While wiretapping obviously assists in apprehending criminals and preventing crime and terrorism, the onus is on those who wish to employ this indiscriminate method of investigation to show that there is an overwhelming need to do so, that it is likely to be effective, and there are no acceptable alternatives. If this cannot be demonstrated, it becomes virtually impossible to justify the practice 'not because we wish to hamper law enforcement, but because there are values we place above efficient police work'.

A prudent approach to the problem would ensure that where the surveillance materials have been acquired in a seriously unconscionable manner, such that it would gravely undermine public confidence in the administration of justice, the information obtained should not be admitted in evidence in court.

# Chapter 4
# **Privacy and free speech**

Supermodel Naomi Campbell was photographed leaving a meeting of Narcotics Anonymous. The British tabloid newspaper *The Daily Mirror* published the pictures, together with articles claiming that she was receiving treatment for her drug addiction. She had denied publicly that she was an addict, and sued the newspaper for damages. The trial court and the Court of Appeal found against her. They held that by mendaciously asserting to the media that she did not take drugs, she had rendered it legitimate for the media to put the record straight. But her appeal to the House of Lords succeeded, and she was awarded compensation for a violation of her privacy.

Photographs of the wedding of Michael Douglas and Catherine Zeta-Jones were surreptitiously taken, notwithstanding explicit notice having been given to all guests forbidding 'photography or video devices at the ceremony or reception'. The couple had entered into an exclusive publication contract with *OK!* magazine, but its rival, *Hello!*, sought to publish these pictures. The stars reached for their lawyers, and won.

The European Court of Human Rights has, on a number of occasions, revealed the inadequacy of European domestic legal protection of privacy. One decision is particularly instructive.

14. Celebrities like supermodel Naomi Campbell are vulnerable
to incessant pursuit by paparazzi

Princess Caroline of Monaco complained that paparazzi employed by several German magazines had photographed her while she was engaged in a variety of quotidian activities, including eating in a restaurant courtyard, horse riding, canoeing, playing with her children, shopping, skiing, kissing a boyfriend, playing tennis, sitting on a beach, and so on. A German court found in her favour in respect of the photographs which, though captured in a public place, were taken when she had 'sought seclusion'.

But, while accepting that some of the pictures were sufficiently intimate to warrant protection (such as those of her with her children or in the company of a boyfriend sitting in a secluded section of a restaurant courtyard), the court dismissed her complaint in regard to the rest. She turned to the European Court, which acknowledged that Article 8 applied, but sought to balance the protection of the princess's private life against that of freedom of expression as guaranteed by Article 10 of the Convention. Taking and publishing photographs, it decided, was a subject in which the protection of an individual's rights and reputation assumed especial significance since it did not concern the dissemination of 'ideas', but of images containing personal, or even intimate, 'information' about that individual. Moreover, pictures published in the tabloid press were frequently snapped in an atmosphere of harassment that generated in the paparazzi's quarry a strong sense of intrusion, or even of persecution.

The critical factor in balancing the protection of private life against freedom of expression, the Court held, was the contribution that the published photographs and articles made to a debate of general interest. The pictures of the princess were, it found, of a purely private nature, taken without her knowledge or consent, and, in some instances, in secret. They made no contribution to a debate of public interest given that she was not engaged in an official function and the photographs and articles related exclusively to details of her private life. Furthermore, while the public might have a right to information, including, in special circumstances, about the private life of public figures, they did not have such a right in this instance. It had no legitimate interest in knowing Princess Caroline's whereabouts or how she behaved in her private life – even in places that could not always be described as secluded. In the same way as there was a commercial interest for the magazines to publish the photographs and articles, those interests had, in the Court's view, to yield to the applicant's right to the effective protection of her private life.

The English courts have recently been vigorously seeking to resolve the endless tussles between public figures and the media. Despite the absence of a privacy statute, the judges appear to have fashioned a remedy out of a cluster of analogous legal actions. This Band-aid is unlikely to yield a coherent or durable solution to the problem.

## Courting publicity?

Celebrities – stars of screen, radio, television, pop music, sport, and the catwalk – are regarded as fair game by the paparazzi. Members of the British royal family – most conspicuously, and tragically, the Princess of Wales – have long been preyed upon by the media.

It is persistently claimed that public figures forfeit their right to privacy. This contention is generally based on the following reasoning. It is asserted that celebrities relish publicity when it is favourable, but resent it when it is hostile. They cannot, it is argued, have it both ways. Second, the opinion is heard that the media have the right to 'put the record straight'. So, in the case of Naomi Campbell, since she lied about her drug addiction, there is, the Court of Appeal held, a public interest in the press revealing the truth.

The first assertion, advanced, not surprisingly, by the media, is a specious application of the idiom: 'live by the sword, die by the

## A bogus public interest?

The argument that adopting a public life forfeits a private life is ridiculous. So too is the argument that, it is reported, many journalists use to establish a public interest: '*anything* may be relevant to assessment of a person's character'. True, anything may be relevant to a person's character, but not everything relevant to a person's character is of public interest. The odious practice of outing homosexuals, for instance, has also been defended on the ground of public interest... Not all persons whose appearance differs from their reality are thereby hypocrites. A homophobe, whether homosexual or not, who acts hostilely towards homosexuals solely because they are homosexuals, is unjust. *That* is the public interest. But if the homophobe is himself also homosexual, to publicize that further fact is protected neither by the outer's freedom of expression nor the public's right to information. On the contrary, it is an outrageous infringement of the homophobe's right to privacy.

James Griffin, *On Human Rights* (Oxford University Press, 2008), pp. 240–1

sword'. It would sound the death knell for the protection of most public figures' private lives. The fact that a celebrity courts publicity – an inescapable feature of fame – cannot be allowed to annihilate their right to shield intimate features of their life from public view.

Nor is the second argument wholly persuasive. Suppose that a celebrity were HIV-positive or suffering from cancer. Can it really be the case that a legitimate desire on his or her part to deny that he or she is a sufferer of one of these diseases may be extinguished by the media's right to 'put the record straight'? If so, the protection of privacy becomes a fragile reed. Truth or falsity should not block the reasonable expectations of those who dwell in the glare of public attention.

But it is not only the rich and famous who have cause for complaint.

## Ordinary people

Mr Peck was deeply depressed. One evening while walking down Brentwood High Street, he attempted to slash his wrists with a kitchen knife. He was unaware that he had been captured on CCTV by a camera installed by Brentwood Borough Council. The CCTV footage did not show him actually cutting his wrists. The operator was alerted only to the image of an individual in possession of a knife. The police were notified and arrived at the scene, where they seized the knife, provided Peck with medical assistance, and transported him to a police station, where he was detained under the Mental Health Act. After being examined and treated by a doctor, he was released without charge and taken home by police officers.

A few months later, the council published two photographs obtained from the CCTV footage to accompany an article headed: 'Defused – the partnership between CCTV and the police prevents a potentially dangerous situation.' Peck's face was not masked. The article described the circumstances as above. A few days afterwards, the *Brentwood Weekly News* used a photograph of the incident on its front page to illustrate an article on the use and benefits of CCTV. Again Peck's face was not concealed. Subsequently, another local newspaper published two similar articles, along with a picture of Peck taken from the CCTV footage, and stated that a potentially dangerous situation had been resolved. It added that Peck had been released without charge. Several readers recognized Peck from the picture.

Then extracts from the CCTV footage were included in a local television programme with an average audience of 350,000. This time, Peck's identity had been obscured, at the Council's oral request. A month or two later, Peck discovered from a neighbour that he had been filmed on CCTV, and that footage had been released. He took no action, as he was still suffering from severe depression.

The CCTV footage was also supplied to the producers of *Crime Beat*, a BBC series on national television with an average of 9.2 million viewers. The Council imposed several conditions, including that nobody should be identifiable in the footage. Nevertheless, trailers for an episode of the programme showed Peck's unmasked face. When friends informed him that they had seen him in the trailers, Peck complained to the Council. It contacted the producers, who confirmed that his image had been covered in the main programme. But when the programme was aired, despite the pixilation, he was recognized by friends and family.

His complaints to the Broadcasting Standards Commission and the Independent Television Commission (both now replaced by Ofcom, the Office of Communications) alleging, among other things, an unwarranted infringement of his privacy, were successful. His objection about the published articles to the Press Complaints Commission was, however, unproductive.

Peck then sought leave from the High Court to apply for judicial review concerning the Council's disclosure of the CCTV material. His application, and a further request for leave to appeal to the Court of Appeal, were both rejected. He therefore pursued his grievance in the European Court, which decided that the disclosure of the CCTV footage by the Council was a disproportionate interference with his private life, contrary to Article 8. The expression 'private life' in the Article was, it held, to be interpreted generously to include the right to identity and personal development.

Merely because the footage was taken on a public street did not render it a public occasion, since Peck was not attending a public event, nor was he a public figure, and it was late at night. Moreover, the disclosure of the footage to the media resulted in its being seen by a significantly larger audience than Peck could reasonably have foreseen. It was the extent of disclosure by the media that breached his Article 8 rights. The Court concluded that the Council could have obtained Mr Peck's consent prior to disclosure and it should have hidden his face.

The case is important authority for the proposition that merely because an individual is in a public place does not render his or her conduct public – except in so far as passers-by witness it. It was the extent of the further disclosure by various forms of media that breached Peck's Article 8 rights.

## Intrusion and disclosure

The pursuit of information by the media frequently requires the use of intrusive methods: deception, zoom lenses, hidden devices, the interception of telephone conversations or correspondence, and the other forms of spying and surveillance described in Chapter 1. There is a tendency to conflate the intrusion practised by the prying journalist with the publication of the information thereby acquired. It is important that the two be kept separate.

This position was sensibly adopted in *Dietemann v Time, Inc.*, in which two reporters of *Life* magazine tricked the plaintiff into allowing them access to his home and there set up hidden surveillance devices to monitor the plaintiff, a virtually uneducated plumber who purported to diagnose and treat physical ailments. The resulting article certainly informed the public about a newsworthy topic – the unlicensed practice of medicine – but the court had to consider whether this would grant immunity to the reporters in respect of their surreptitious newsgathering techniques. On appeal, the judgment in the plaintiff's favour for invasion of privacy was upheld. In answer to the defendant's claim that the First Amendment's shield extended not only to publication but to investigation, the court remarked that the amendment 'has never been construed to accord newsmen immunity from torts or crimes committed during the course of newsgathering'.

Significantly, in its assessment of damages, the court took into account not only the nature and extent of the intrusive acts, but also the publication. It noted that 'there is no First Amendment interest in protecting news media from calculated misdeeds [thus] damages for intrusion [may] be enhanced by the fact of later publication'.

In respect of the First Amendment, though, the 'right to gather information is logically antecedent and practically necessary to any exercise of [the right to publish] and . . . cannot be given full meaning unless that antecedent right is recognized'. The common law denies the media a general privilege to gather information. Accordingly, the court correctly separated the two questions of intrusion and disclosure, assessing the reasonableness of the defendants' newsgathering techniques in the light of the common law principles developed under the former, and eschewing any First Amendment argument which would inevitably influence the latter.

The answer lies in the formulation of independent criteria by which to assess when an individual's seclusion may justifiably be violated, just as there are standards by which to test when the disclosure of private facts may be justified in the public interest.

## Freedom of expression

We are all publishers now. The Internet has created hitherto unthinkable opportunities for freedom of expression. Bloggers proliferate at the rate of 120,000 a day. Social networking is the new form of community; Facebook has some 300 million members,

joyoftech.com

**15. Revealing personal information is often hard to resist**

MySpace around 100 million. Yet, these astonishing developments notwithstanding, the central question remains the same. How is privacy to be reconciled with freedom of expression?

The electronic age has still to address Warren and Brandeis's entreaty (discussed in Chapter 3) that the law ought to prevent the distress caused by the gratuitous publication of private information.

What are the justifications for free speech in a democratic society? They tend to be based either on the positive consequences fostered by the exercise of the freedom, or on the protection of individuals' right to express themselves. The former – consequentialist – argument

### Gossip online

Even if gossip in cyberspace never bubbles up into the traditional press, it is more widely broadcast and more easily misinterpreted than it is in real space, resurrecting all of the stifling intimacy of a traditional society without the redeeming promise of being judged in context. The fact that gossip in cyberspace is recorded, permanently retrievable, and globally accessible increases the risk that an individual's public face will be threatened by past indiscretions. Gossip published on an Internet chat group may, in the short run, reach an audience that is no bigger than gossip over the back fence in a small town. But because Internet gossip, unlike individual memories, never fades, it can be resurrected in the future by those who don't know the individual in question, and thus are unable to put the information in a larger context. And unlike gossip in a small town, Internet gossip is hard to answer, because its potential audience is anonymous and unbounded.

Jeffrey Rosen, *The Unwanted Gaze: The Destruction of Privacy in America* (Random House, 2000), p. 205

usually draws on the case made for free speech by John Milton and John Stuart Mill. The latter – rights-based – argument conceives of speech as an integral part of an individual's right to self-fulfilment.

These principles tend invariably to be amalgamated, and even confused. So, for example, Thomas Emerson discerns the following four primary justifications which include both sorts of claim: individual self-fulfilment; attainment of the truth; securing the participation by members of society in social, including political, decision-making; and providing the means of maintaining the balance between stability and change in society.

Champions of privacy, on the other hand, rely almost exclusively on rights-based arguments, as outlined in Chapter 2. But the extent to which the law may legitimately curtail speech that undermines an individual's privacy is often presented as a contest between these two heavyweights: freedom of speech versus privacy. But this may be mere shadow boxing. Why? Because 'at most points the law of privacy and the law sustaining a free press do not contradict each other. On the contrary, they are mutually supportive, in that both are vital features of the basic system of individual rights.'

## A better approach?

The mist begins to clear once we focus our attention on the essential nature of privacy. When it is recognized that our core concern is the protection of personal information, the real character of the debate is illuminated. Happily (though all too rarely), from within the dark depths of the voluminous literature, shafts of light appear. For example, after a detailed discussion of the public disclosure tort, one writer concludes:

> Privacy law might be more just and effective if it were to focus on identifying (preferably by statute) those exchanges of information that warrant protection at their point of origin, rather than continuing its current, capricious course of imposing liability only if the material is ultimately disseminated to the public at large ... [A] careful identification of particularly sensitive situations in which personal information is exchanged, and an equally careful delineation of the appropriate expectations regarding how that information can be used, could significantly curtail abuses without seriously hampering freedom of speech. At the very least, this possibility merits considerably more thought as an alternative to the Warren and Brandeis tort than it has received thus far.

And even Thomas Emerson suggests that there might be
'[a]nother approach, and one that seems to me to be more fruitful'
that would:

> place more emphasis on developing the privacy side of the balance.
> It would recognise the first amendment interests but it would give
> primary attention to a number of factors which derive ultimately
> from the functions performed by privacy and the expectations of
> privacy that prevail in contemporary society.

The first such factor is:

> [T]he element of intimacy in determining the zone of privacy. Thus
> so far as the privacy tort [of public disclosure] is concerned,
> protection would be extended only to matters related to the intimate
> details of a person's life: those activities, ideas or emotions which
> one does not share with others or shares only with those who are
> closest. This would include sexual relations, the performance of
> bodily functions, family relations, and the like.

There are some positive signs therefore that the quest for the
elusive equilibrium between privacy and free speech has produced
some scepticism about the conventional approach that languishes
in an incoherent concept of privacy.

## Whose freedom?

Does freedom of speech protect the interests of the speaker or
the listener? Or, to put it more portentously, is the justification
individual- or community-based?

The former is rights-based, and argues for the interests in
individual autonomy, dignity, self-fulfilment, and other values that
the exercise of free speech safeguards or advances. The latter is
community-based, and is consequentialist or utilitarian. It draws

on democratic theory or the promotion of truth to support free speech as facilitating or encouraging the unfettered exchange of ideas, the dissemination of information, and other means of enlarging participation in self-government.

Freedom of speech and privacy are often regarded as rights or interests of the individual, and – sometimes in the same breath – as rights or interests of the community as a whole. And, even more troubling, free speech is regarded as one, and privacy the other, thereby rendering any 'balancing' of the two somewhat problematic! In respect of the interests of the individual, they generally share the same concerns. Indeed, the social functions of privacy are difficult to distinguish from those of freedom of expression, as mentioned above. To treat them both as individual rights would seem to be an important step towards simplifying the issue.

## Policy and principle

Theories of freedom of expression that seek to protect the audience are generally arguments of policy, based on the importance of that freedom to the community. Those that advance the interests of the speaker, on the other hand, are generally arguments of principle which give primacy to the individual's self-fulfilment over the interests of the community. The jurist Ronald Dworkin has suggested that free speech is likely to receive stronger protection when it is regarded as safeguarding, as a matter of principle, the rights of the speaker. And privacy is, in its broad sense, also rights-based rather than goal-based. If this is correct, it would at least facilitate a greater symmetry in the balancing exercise.

Unfortunately, the matter is more complex. At first blush, this strategy would provide a logical basis for claiming that publications that harm other individuals cannot seriously be said to advance the speaker's or publisher's interest in self-fulfilment. Who is 'fulfilled' by the disclosure that a supermodel is a drug addict? And who is to say whether certain forms of speech are instrumental in achieving this object?

Moreover, the argument 'suffers from a failure to distinguish intellectual self-fulfilment from other wants and needs, and thus fails to support a distinct principle of free speech'. It is also founded on the principle of the free dissemination of *ideas* rather than *information*, which reduces its utility in the present context. And, most embarrassingly, the argument is hard to deploy in defence of *press* freedom, which appears to rest almost entirely on the interests of the community, rather than the individual journalist, editor, or publisher.

What of the speaker's motives? It would not be unduly disingenuous to suggest that profit may be of some interest to newspaper editors and proprietors. And, as Eric Barendt remarks, 'a rigorous examination of motives to exclude speech made for profit would leave little immune from regulation'. Nor does the audience necessarily care; a good read is a good read whether its author is moved by greed or edification.

## Truth

John Stuart Mill's celebrated argument from truth is based on the idea that any suppression of speech is an 'assumption of infallibility' and that only by the unrestricted circulation of ideas can the truth be revealed. But when taken to its logical conclusion, this would prevent any inroads being made into the exercise of the right to speak – at least truthfully. Apart from Mill's dubious supposition that there is an objective 'truth' out there, and his confidence in the dominance of reason, his theory makes the legal regulation of disclosures of personal information (as well as several other forms of speech that cause harm) extremely difficult to justify. It asserts that freedom of expression is a social good because it is the best process by which to advance knowledge

### Truth versus falsehood

And though all the winds of doctrine were let loose to play on the earth, so Truth be in the field, we do injuriously by licensing and prohibiting misdoubt her strength. Let her and Falsehood grapple; who ever knew Truth put to the worse in a free and open encounter?

I cannot praise a fugitive and cloistered virtue, unexercised and unbreathed, that never sallies out and sees her adversary, but slinks out of the race, where that immortal garland is to be run for, not without dust and heat.

John Milton, *Areopagitica* (1644) (MacMillan, 1915)

and discover truth, starting from the premise that the soundest and most rational judgment is arrived at by considering all facts and arguments for and against. And, according to Emerson, this free marketplace of ideas should exist irrespective of how pernicious or false the new opinion appears to be 'because there is no way of suppressing the false without suppressing the true'.

But is the argument from truth really relevant to the protection of privacy? Frederick Schauer doubts whether truth is indeed ultimate and non-instrumental; does it not secure a 'deeper good' such as happiness or dignity? If truth is instrumental, then whether more truth causes a consequential strengthening of this deeper good is a question of fact and not an inexorable, logical certainty from definition. For Schauer, the argument from truth is an 'argument from knowledge'; an argument that the value in question is having people believe that things are in fact true.

## Democracy

Free speech performs an essential function in promoting and maintaining democratic self-governance. This is an extension of

the argument from truth, as the American political theorist
Alexander Meiklejohn puts it:

> The principle of the freedom of speech springs from the necessities
> of the program of self-government. It is not a Law of Nature or
> Reason in the abstract. It is a deduction from the basic American
> agreement that public issues shall be decided by universal suffrage.

Yet, as in the case of the argument from truth, it must be queried
how self-government is facilitated or advanced by the revelation of
intimate private facts about, say, an individual's sexual proclivities?
Is it 'speech' at all?

In some cases, such information may be relevant to self-
government. Where, for instance, people acting through their
democratically elected government consider a certain action to be
sufficiently antisocial to constitute a criminal offence, then it is in
the interest of self-governance that offenders are apprehended and
punished. Similarly, where an individual holds a public office, and
thereby actually acts on behalf of the people, representing and
implementing their political opinions, any activity of that person
which pertains directly to his or her fitness to perform that
function is a legitimate interest of the community. Sadly, there are
all too many examples of politicians championing 'family values',
who are then exposed as adulterers or worse. A public interest test
is capable of supporting freedom of expression in these cases. The
argument from democracy should not be taken to justify unlimited
freedom of speech in the privacy arena.

## Press freedom

Arguments from democracy are in full flower here. For Milton and
Blackstone, it was the prior restraint of the press that represented
the most sinister threat to freedom of speech. Sir William
Blackstone, the 18th-century jurist, declared:

The liberty of the press is indeed essential to the nature of a free state; but this consists in laying no previous restraints upon publications and not in freedom from censure for criminal matter when published. Every free man has an undoubted right to lay what sentiments he pleases before the public: to forbid this, is to destroy the freedom of the press: but if he publishes what is improper, mischievous, or illegal, he must take the consequence of his own temerity.

Both the conception of the press and the boundaries of its freedom are, however, considerably wider today. Thus the term 'press' normally extends beyond newspapers and periodicals, and includes a far wider range of publications media: television, radio, and the Internet. Nor is the scope of press freedom restricted to prohibitions against 'prior constraint'.

The political justification for free speech is an application of the argument from truth. Mill's second hypothesis, it will be recalled, is the 'assumption of infallibility' that specifies the conditions under which we are able to have confidence in believing that what we think is true, actually is true. The safest way to achieve this, the argument runs, is to accord individuals the freedom to debate ideas: to subject them to contradiction and refutation. Interference with this freedom diminishes our ability to arrive at rational beliefs.

This is a powerful idea, even if it may appear to be based on an idealized model of the political process in which there is active popular participation in government. A free press does have the potential to engender this awareness and to facilitate its exercise.

The appeal of the arguments from truth and from democracy is that they establish independent grounds for freedom of expression in a way that arguments based on the interests of the speaker do not. But the media publish much that, even by the most generous exercise of the imagination, is not remotely connected to these noble pursuits. Does this suggest that they are entitled to no special treatment? Arguments to support special treatment for the press tend to fall on stony judicial ground. A stronger case can plainly be made where, unlike the *Daily Mirror* in the Naomi Campbell case, the press offends decorum rather than the law. This argument may then be made to turn on the importance to the political process of the publication of a particular report. Accounts of the private lives of government ministers, officials, politicians, and even perhaps royalty, it could plausibly be claimed, warrant special treatment. Here, the nature of the message, and not the medium of its propagation, is the focal point of concern. This approach does not distinguish whether the freedom is exercised in the press or the pub. It has the additional merit of avoiding the problem of defining the 'press'.

## The First Amendment

In the United States, the issue of freedom of expression is debated against the background of the First Amendment's injunction that 'Congress shall make no law … abridging the freedom of speech, or of the press'. American courts and commentators have developed several theories of free speech, both rights-based and consequentialist, which seek to account for the exercise of freedom of expression in all its protean forms. Nevertheless, though it would be artificial to conceive of the problems encountered by the efforts to reconcile privacy and free speech as a discrete matter, the American law does appear to have developed the contours of a privacy/free speech theory.

In particular, there is a tendency to adopt a purposive construction of the First Amendment. This asks: what forms of speech or publication warrant protection by virtue of their contribution to the operation of political democracy. It has been employed in several decisions that distinguish, with variable consequences, between public figures and ordinary individuals. Indeed, the

Supreme Court applied the principle adopted in the well-known libel case of *New York Times v Sullivan* to the privacy case of *Time, Inc. v Hill* (see below). In the former decision, the Court expressed its philosophy in unequivocal terms:

> [W]e consider this case against the background of a profound national commitment to the principle that debate on public issues should be uninhibited, robust and wide open, and that it may well include vehement, caustic, and sometimes unpleasantly sharp attacks on government and public officials.

The chief purpose of the First Amendment is, in this approach, the protection of the right of all citizens to understand political issues in order that they might participate effectively in the operation of democratic government. This formula allows considerable scope for actions by private individuals who have been subjected to gratuitous publicity. In practice, however, it is frequently those who are in the public eye that – for this very reason – attract the attention of the tabloids. The difficult question which the theory is then required to answer is the extent to which such public figures are entitled to protection of aspects of their personal lives. And this, in turn, involves a delicate investigation of what features of a public figure's life may legitimately be exposed – in the furtherance of political debate. His sex life? Her health? Their finances?

Although this theory seeks to distinguish between voluntary and involuntary public figures, its application, except as a general rationale for the existence of the freedom of speech itself, provides uncertain guidance as to the respective rights and obligations in cases involving unwanted publicity. In the absence of an attempt to define the kinds of information in respect of which all individuals might *prima facie* expect to receive protection (even if such protection is subsequently to be outweighed by considerations of the public interest), one of the central purposes of recognizing an individual's interest in restricting information – the trust, candour, and confidence it fosters – is diminished.

## Balancing competing interests

Is it possible to formulate a coherent theory of free speech which is both sufficiently broad to capture the complexities of the exercise of the freedom, and sufficiently specific to account for its variable applications? The argument from democracy attracts greater support than the Millian or autonomy-based theories, but all provide at best only the most general guidance in respect of the legitimate controls on the public disclosure of personal information by the media.

An interest-based theory that specifies the particular interests of the parties involved in the disclosure raises numerous difficulties (not unlike the interest-based accounts of privacy). And, while it is useful to distinguish, say, the 'personality' interests involved when private facts are published from the 'reputational' interests affected by defamatory publications, or the 'commercial' interests affected by breaches of confidence, this approach fails to explain which species of information warrant protection in the face of the competing claims of free speech.

The American Supreme Court has, in mediating between the two interests, resorted to the process of 'balancing' by which the interest in free speech is weighed against other interests such as national security, public order, and so on. If such interests are found to be 'compelling' or 'substantial', or where there is a 'clear and present danger' that the speech will cause significant harm to the public interest, the Court will uphold the restriction of free speech.

## The dynamics of limitation

Emerson uses this phrase to describe the proposition that the public interest in the freedom of expression must fit in to a 'more comprehensive scheme of social values and social goals'. So far,

I have touched on the inapplicability of certain free speech justifications; I have allowed the right of privacy to escape unscathed. Where there is a genuine conflict between the two values how is privacy to be protected? Or, in other words, why should free speech be subordinated to the protection of personal information?

In what circumstances might the absolute protection of free speech be moderated? Emerson suggests three. The first is where the injury is direct and peculiar to the individual, rather than one suffered in common with others. The second is when the interest is an intimate and personal one: embracing an area of privacy from which both the state and other individuals should be excluded. The third consideration is whether or not society leaves the burden of protecting the interest to the individual, by, for example recognizing that he or she has a legal cause of action.

In the first two circumstances, the harm is likely to be direct and irremediable. Moreover, if the individual has the burden of establishing his or her case, the resources of the state are less likely to be marshalled into a coherent apparatus for the restriction of free speech. He proposes that 'so long as the interest of privacy is genuine, the conditions of recovery clearly defined, and the remedy left to the individual suit, it is most unlikely that the balance will be tipped too far toward restriction of expression'.

Even against the background of the First Amendment, Emerson's approach is persuasive. And no less so in the context of the English law's constitutional silences as to safeguards for free speech. In the words of one senior judge:

> It cannot be too strongly emphasised that outside the established
> exceptions, or any new ones which Parliament may enact in
> accordance with its obligations under the Convention [for the
> Protection of Human Rights and Fundamental Freedoms], there is

no question of balancing freedom of speech against other interests.
It is a trump card which always wins.

The court nevertheless acknowledged, that 'a right of privacy may
be a legitimate exception to freedom of speech'. And other judges
have recognized that there are 'exceptional cases, where the
intended publication is plainly unlawful and would inflict grave
injury on innocent people or seriously impede the course of justice'
Another declared that 'Blackstone was concerned to prevent
government interference with the press. The times of Blackstone
are not relevant to the times of Mr Murdoch.'

## The public interest

When is a matter in the public interest? Courts have struggled to
formulate rational criteria by which to make this controversial
judgment. Among the considerations that would seem to be
relevant are the following: To whom was the information given? Is
the victim a public figure? Was he or she in a public place? Is the
information in the public domain? Did the victim consent to
publication? How was the information acquired? Was it essential
for the victim's identity to be revealed? Was the invasion a serious
one? What were the publisher's motives in disclosing the
information?

In the United States, publishers need only to raise the defence of
public interest or newsworthiness for it generally to demolish the
protection against the gratuitous publication of private facts by the
media. Thus in *Sidis*, the court declared that 'at some point the
public interest in obtaining information becomes dominant over
the individual's desire for privacy'. The privilege is defined in the
*Second Restatement of Torts* as extending to information 'of
legitimate concern to the public' – a conclusion which is reached by
weighing the competing interests of the public's right to know
against the individual's right to keep private facts from the public's

gaze. This may be decided by the judge, as a matter of law or, more often, by the jury as a question of fact. The test embodied in the *Restatement*, reads as follows:

> In determining what comprises a matter of legitimate public interest, account must be taken of the customs and conventions of the community; and in the last analysis what is proper becomes a matter of the community mores. The line is to be drawn when the publicity ceases to be the giving of information to which the public is entitled, and becomes a morbid and sensational prying into private lives for its own sake, with which a reasonable member of the public, with decent standards, would say that he had no concern.

The categories of information which are newsworthy have steadily expanded as the courts have become increasingly conscious of the free speech implications of censoring accurate reporting. Sexual matters – understandably – dominate. This is illustrated by two Californian cases. In the first, an ex-marine became the subject of intense media interest when he foiled an assassination attempt on President Ford. The *San Francisco Chronicle* revealed that Sipple was a prominent member of the gay community, which indeed was true, but he brought an action under the tort of the public disclosure of private facts because he claimed that he had always kept his homosexuality private from his relatives. The court dismissed his action on two grounds. First, the information was already in the public domain, and, second, it held that the facts disclosed were newsworthy because the exposé was fuelled by the wish to combat the stereotyping of gays as 'timid, weak and unheroic', and to discuss the potential biases of the President (one newspaper had suggested that the President's reticence in thanking Sipple was on account of the latter's homosexuality).

In the other case, a newspaper article revealed that the first female student president of a Californian college, Diaz, was a transsexual. The court held that her transsexuality was a private fact and also that, although she was involved in a public controversy (in that she accused the college of misuse of student funds), the disclosure was irrelevant to that issue and, accordingly, not newsworthy. The court emphasized that the purpose of First Amendment protection was 'to keep the public informed so that they may make intelligent decisions on matters important to self-governing people'. It was further explained that 'the fact that she is a transsexual does not adversely reflect on her honesty or judgment. Nor does the fact that she was the first woman student body president, in itself, warrant that her entire private life be open to public inspection.'

How are these two decisions to be reconciled? The answer may lie in the tenor of the *Diaz* article. The newspaper argued that the report was intended to portray the 'changing roles of women in society', but it was clear from the tone of the article that the author's objective stopped at the 'stark revelation'. An important feature of both decisions is that the articles purported to portray alternative lifestyles. It is therefore arguable that, if the article about Diaz had seriously intended to portray the changing role of women in society, the court may have resisted calls for its censorship.

## Celebrities

Our planet is star-struck. The most trivial item of gossip about a celebrity seems to excite huge interest and fascination. News stands are crammed with magazines devoted to the unremitting supply of these ephemeral, generally inane, facts. Does stardom extinguish privacy? Though the *American Restatement* comments that 'there may be some intimate details of her life, such as sexual relations, which even the actress is entitled to keep to herself', the decision in *Ann-Margret v High Society Magazine, Inc.* illustrates that this delicacy has not yet been embraced by the courts. In that case, the actress was denied relief in respect of the publication of a nude photograph of herself, partly because the photograph was of 'a woman who has occupied the fantasies of many movie-goers' and therefore 'of great interest to many people'.

It is often claimed that courts simply accept the judgment of the press as to what is newsworthy. One writer contends that 'deference to the judgment of the press may actually be the appropriate and principled response to the newsworthiness enquiry'. But this neglects the reason why the subject is contentious at all. She observes that 'the economic survival of publishers and broadcasters depends upon their ability to provide a product that the public will buy', and argues that marketplace competition breeds into the papers a 'responsiveness to what substantial segments of the population want to know to cope with the society in which they live'.

The concept of public interest all too easily camouflages the commercial motives of the media. Worse, it masquerades as the democratic exercise of consumer choice: we get the sensationalism we deserve. Both forms of cynical tabloidism neglect the consequences for individuals who happen to be public figures because they are unfortunate enough to be catapulted into the public eye.

## A mores test

To evaluate what is 'highly offensive', the American courts have developed what has been called a 'mores test'. Thus, in *Melvin v Reid*, the plaintiff's past as a prostitute and defendant in a sensational murder trial was revealed in a film called *The Red Kimono* which was based on these events. She had, in the eight years since her acquittal, been accepted into 'respectable society', married, and moved in a circle of friends who were ignorant of her past. Her action for the invasion of her privacy caused by the defendant's truthful disclosures was sustained by the California court (which had not hitherto recognized an action for invasion of privacy).

In *Sidis v F.-R. Publishing Corporation*, on the other hand, the plaintiff, a former child prodigy who, at 11, lectured in mathematics at Harvard, had become a recluse and devoted his time to studying the Okamakammessett Indians and collecting streetcar transfers. The *New Yorker* published an article, 'Where Are They Now? April Fool' written by James Thurber under a pseudonym. Details of Sidis's physical characteristics and mannerisms, the single room in which he lived, and his current activities were revealed. The magazine article acknowledged that Sidis had informed the reporter who had tracked him down for the interview that he lived in fear of publicity and changed jobs whenever his employer or fellow workers learned of his past. The New York District Court denied his action for invasion of privacy on the ground that it could find no decision 'which held the "right of privacy" to be violated by a newspaper or magazine publishing a correct account of one's life or doings . . . except under abnormal circumstances which did not exist in the case at bar'. On appeal, the Second Circuit affirmed the dismissal of the privacy action, but appeared to base its decision on a balancing of the offensiveness of the article with the public or private character of the plaintiff.

In neither *Melvin* nor *Sidis* however, was there a proper attempt to consider the extent to which the information divulged was 'private'. The conceptually vague notions of 'community customs', 'newsworthiness', and the 'offensiveness' of the publication, render these and many other decisions concerning 'public disclosure' unhelpful in an area of considerable constitutional importance. And this is equally true of the efforts by the Supreme Court to fix the boundaries of the First Amendment in respect of publications which affect the plaintiff's privacy. For example, in *Time, Inc. v Hill* the Court held that the plaintiff's action for invasion of privacy failed where he (and his family) had been the subject of a substantially false report. The defendant had published a description of a new play adapted from a novel which fictionalized the ordeal suffered by the plaintiff when he and his family were held hostage in their home by a group of escaped prisoners.

Adopting the test that it had applied in respect of defamation, the Supreme Court held, by a majority, that unless there was proof of actual malice (i.e. that the defendant knowingly published an untrue report), the action would fail. Falsity alone did not deprive the defendant of his protection under the First Amendment – if the publication was newsworthy. And, since the 'opening of a new play linked to an actual incident is a matter of public interest', the plaintiff, because he was unable to show malice, failed. Yet it does seem that the decision was not really concerned with the public disclosure of private information—whether or not it was even a genuine libel action!

## The future

There is no golden fleece. Enactment tomorrow anywhere of a comprehensive privacy statute would generate new problems for the judicial construction of victims' rights against unsolicited intrusions into private lives. Nor would these difficulties be diminished if the courts were to pursue a common law case-by-case route toward protection. The media would continue to be tested daily – with more concentrated minds perhaps – as to whether stories are in the 'public interest'.

The quest for a just equilibrium will never end. The key issue is whether, as often seems to be the case, the interests of the individual are to be sacrificed at the altar of a contrived public interest? Opponents of legal, or even non-legal, checks on unwanted public disclosure like to depict concern for the victim as quaint or prudish. This is distinguished from the vigorous pursuit of the truth by the media. In many cases, of course, newspapers, like all commercial institutions, are moved by the interests of their shareholders, who may be less concerned about what is published in the paper than what appears in its balance sheet. Nor, since the press frequently concedes that it should resist publishing insensitive disclosures of private facts, it is hardly in a position to characterize such apprehensions as pious or censorious.

Privacy advocates may well include enemies of free speech, but that is no more a legitimate argument against them than the contention that advocates of free speech include avaricious newspaper proprietors. The power of the press lobby can, however, never be underestimated. How many politicians, whose careers often hang by a slender thread, wish to invite the animosity of the tabloids by championing curbs on reporting of what has come to be called 'bonk journalism'? The press, while quick to condemn the exposure of private lives in the name of the public interest, inevitably closes ranks against legislation. Unhappily, while most tabloids preach family values, they often demonstrate little concern or respect for the families of their victims.

# Chapter 5
# **Data protection**

Information is no longer merely power. It is big business. In recent years, the fastest growing component of international trade has been the service sector. It accounts for more than a third of world trade – and continues to expand. It is a commonplace to identify, as a central feature of modern industrialized societies, their dependence on the storage of information. The use of computers facilitates, of course, considerably greater efficiency and velocity in the collection, storage, use, retrieval, and transfer of information.

The routine functions of government and private institutions require a constant stream of data about us in order to administer effectively the countless services that are an essential ingredient of contemporary life. The provision of health services, social security, credit, insurance, and the prevention and detection of crime assume the availability of a substantial quantity of personal data and, hence, a readiness by individuals to supply it. The computerization of this – often highly sensitive – information intensifies the risks of its misuse.

Or indeed its careless loss. For example, Britain has recently experienced a number of security scandals. In 2008, a computer memory stick containing information on thousands of criminals was lost. On another occasion documents relating to al-Qaeda in Pakistan and the security situation in Iraq were left on a train by a Cabinet Office intelligence official. In 2007, the Chancellor of the Exchequer confessed that computer disks holding personal information on 25 million individuals and 7.2 million families had disappeared.

## Genesis

The dawn of information technology in the 1960s witnessed growing anxiety about the perceived threats posed by the uncontrolled collection, storage, and use of personal data. The fear of Big Brother provoked calls in several countries for the regulation of these potentially intrusive activities. The first data-protection law was enacted in the German Land of Hesse in 1970. This was followed by national legislation in Sweden (1973), the United States (1974), Germany (1977), and France (1978).

Out of this early chrysalis were born two key international instruments: the Council of Europe's 1981 Convention for the Protection of Individuals with regard to the Automatic Processing of Personal Data, and the 1980 Organization for Economic Cooperation and Development (OECD) Guidelines Governing the Protection of Privacy and Transborder Data Flows of Personal Data. These documents formulated explicit rules governing the complete process of managing electronic data. At the core of data-protection legislation, since the OECD guidelines, is the proposition that data relating to an identifiable individual should not be collected in the absence of a genuine purpose and the consent of the individual concerned (see box).

At a slightly higher level of abstraction, it encapsulates the principle of what the German Constitutional Court has called 'informational self-determination' – an ideal that expresses a fundamental democratic ideal.

# The OECD principles

## Collection Limitation Principle

There should be limits to the collection of personal data and any such data should be obtained by lawful and fair means and, where appropriate, with the knowledge or consent of the data subject.

## Data Quality Principle

Personal data should be relevant to the purposes for which they are to be used, and, to the extent necessary for those purposes, should be accurate, complete and kept up-to-date.

## Purpose Specification Principle

The purposes for which personal data are collected should be specified not later than at the time of data collection and the subsequent use limited to the fulfilment of those purposes or such others as are not incompatible with those purposes and as are specified on each occasion of change of purpose.

## Use Limitation Principle

Personal data should not be disclosed, made available or otherwise used for purposes other than those specified in accordance with Paragraph 9 except:
a)   with the consent of the data subject; or
b)   by the authority of law.

## Security Safeguards Principle

Personal data should be protected by reasonable security safeguards against such risks as loss or unauthorized access, destruction, use, modification or disclosure of data.

## Openness Principle

There should be a general policy of openness about developments, practices and policies with respect to personal data. Means should be readily available of establishing the existence and nature of personal data, and the main purposes of their use, as well as the identity and usual residence of the data controller.

## Individual Participation Principle

An individual should have the right:

a) to obtain from a data controller, or otherwise, confirmation of whether or not the data controller has data relating to him;

b) to have communicated to him, data relating to him

(i) within a reasonable time;

(ii) at a charge, if any, that is not excessive;

(iii) in a reasonable manner; and

(iv) in a form that is readily intelligible to him;

c) to be given reasons if a request made under subparagraphs (a) and (b) is denied, and to be able to challenge such denial; and

d) to challenge data relating to him and, if the challenge is successful to have the data erased, rectified, completed or amended.

## Accountability Principle

A data controller should be accountable for complying with measures which give effect to the principles stated above.

OECD Guidelines on the Protection of Privacy and Transborder Flows of Personal Data, Part Two (adopted 23 September 1980)

Adherence to, or more precisely, enforcement of, this objective (and the associated rights of access and correction) has been mixed in the forty or so jurisdictions that have enacted data-protection legislation. Most of these statutes draw on the two international instruments mentioned above. Article 1 of the Council of Europe's Convention on the Protection of Individuals with Regard to Automatic Processing of Personal Data states that its purpose is to secure in the territory of each Party for every individual, whatever his nationality or residence, respect for his rights and fundamental freedoms, and in particular his right to privacy, with regard to automatic processing of personal data relating to him ('data protection').

The importance of these principles cannot be overstated. In particular, of the use limitation and purpose specification principles are crucial canons of fair information practice. Together with the principle that personal data shall be collected by means that are fair and lawful, they provide a framework for safeguarding the use and disclosure of such data, but also (in the fair collection principle) for limiting intrusive activities such as the interception of email messages. Personal data may be used or disclosed only for the purposes for which the data were collected or for some directly related purposes, unless the data subject consents. This key precept goes a long way towards regulating the misuse of personal data on the Internet. But it requires rejuvenation where it already exists and urgent adoption where it does so only partially (most conspicuously in the United States).

The enactment of data-protection legislation is driven only partly by altruism. The new information technology disintegrates national borders; international traffic in personal data is a routine feature of commercial life. The protection afforded to personal data in Country A is, in a digital world, rendered nugatory when it is retrieved on a computer in Country B in which there are no controls over its use. Hence, states with data-protection laws frequently proscribe the transfer of data to countries that lack them. Indeed, the European Union has in one of its several directives explicitly sought to annihilate these 'data havens'. Without data-protection legislation, countries risk being shut out of the rapidly expanding information business.

# EU Directive on the processing of personal data

## Article 3

1. This Directive shall apply to the processing of personal data wholly or partly by automatic means, and to the processing otherwise than by automatic means of personal data which form part of a filing system or are intended to form part of a filing system.

2. This Directive shall not apply to the processing of personal data: in the course of an activity which falls outside the scope of Community law, . . . and in any case to processing operations concerning public security, defence, State security (including the economic well-being of the State when the processing operation relates to State security matters) and the activities of the State in areas of criminal law, by a natural person in the course of a purely personal or household activity.

## Article 6

1. Membering States shall provide that personal data must be:
   (a) processed fairly and lawfully;
   (b) collected for specified, explicit and legitimate purposes and not further processed in a way incompatible with those purposes. Further processing of data for historical, statistical or scientific purposes shall not be considered as incompatible provided that Member States provide appropriate safeguards;
   (c) adequate, relevant and not excessive in relation to the purposes for which they are collected and/or further processed;
   (d) accurate and, where necessary, kept up to date; every reasonable step must be taken to ensure that data which are inaccurate or incomplete, having regard to the purposes for which they were collected or for which they are further processed, are erased or rectified;

## The essentials of data protection

At the heart of any data-protection law lies the principle that
personal data shall be collected by means that are 'lawful and fair
in the circumstances of the case', to use the language of Hong
Kong's Personal Data (Privacy) Ordinance of 1995 that will serve
as a paradigm here. In respect of the use and disclosure of such
data, they may be used or disclosed for the purposes for which the
data were collected or for some directly related purposes, unless
the data subject consents.

These provisions are buttressed by six 'data-protection principles'
which are, in effect, the main cog of the legislative machinery.
Briefly, the first principle prohibits the collection of data unless
they are collected for a lawful purpose directly related to a function
or activity of the data user who is to use the data, and that are
adequate but not excessive in relation to that purpose. Personal
data may be collected only by lawful and fair means. This requires a
data user to inform the data subject of the purpose for which the
data are to be used, the classes of persons to whom the data may be
transferred, whether it is obligatory or voluntary for the data
subject to supply the data, the consequences of failure to supply the
data; and that the data subject has the right to request access to
and correction of the data.

second principle requires data users to ensure that the data
are accurate and up to date. If in doubt, the data user should

discontinue using the data at once. It should not retain the data any longer than is necessary for the purpose for which they were collected. The third principle provides that without the prescribed consent of the data subject, personal data may not be used for any purpose other than the purpose for which the data were to be used at the time of their collection.

Fourth, data users are obliged to take appropriate security measures to protect personal data. They must ensure that they are adequately protected against unauthorized or accidental access, processing, erasure, or use by others lacking authority. The fifth principle relates to the publicity a data user is required to give to the kind of personal data it holds, and its policies and practices in respect of the handling of personal data. This is normally achieved by a 'privacy policy statement' that includes details of the accuracy, retention period, security, and use of the data, as well as measures taken regarding data access and data correction requests.

The final principle relates to the data subject's right to obtain access to personal data about him or her and to request a copy of such personal data held by that data user. Should the data turn out to be inaccurate, the data subject has the right to request the data user to correct the record.

A victim of intrusion or disclosure may complain to the Privacy Commissioner for Personal Data of a contravention of these principles. He or she has the power to issue an 'enforcement notice' to compel compliance with the law. Failure to comply with such a notice is an offence punishable on conviction by a fine and two years' imprisonment. The legislation provides also for compensation, including damages for injury to feelings.

A crucial element of the law is the power vested in the Privacy Commissioner to approve codes of practice to provide 'practical guidance' to both data users and data subjects. Those issued so far by the Commissioner are substantial documents that are a product of detailed and lengthy consultation with the appropriate parties. Moreover, while the statute provides that a failure by a data user to observe any part of a code shall not render it liable to civil or criminal proceedings, an allegation in such proceedings that a data user has failed to follow the code is admissible as evidence.

## What are 'personal data'?

The starting point of any data-protection law is the concept of 'personal data' or, in some statutes, 'personal information'. The term has been used numerous times in this book, but what precisely does it include? Though there are differences between domestic statutes, they share a fairly broadly defined notion of the phrase. Article 2(a) of the European Union Directive employs the following formulation:

> [A]ny information relating to an identified or identifiable individual natural person ('data subject'); an identifiable individual is one who can be identified directly or indirectly, in particular by reference to an identification number or to one or more factors specific to his physical, physiological, mental, economic, cultural or social identity.

But what of data generated by cookies or RFID tags embedded in products or clothing? They do not necessarily refer to an individual, but since they facilitate decisions about a person, they warrant protection under the rubric of personal data.

Though the definition of personal data in existing legislation manifestly incorporates information the obtaining or disclosure of which would constitute what might properly be called an invasion of privacy, its wide sweep neglects these issues. My own view is that it is principally information that is intimate or confidential that warrants protection in the name of privacy. But while the Directive, and domestic data-protection legislation, neglects this species of information, it does not altogether ignore it, as we shall see.

Despite the fact that any data-protection regime extends well beyond the information of an essentially private kind, and their (perhaps inevitable) procedural, rather than substantive, nature, they provide useful signposts to the more effective resolution of the challenges, especially of electronic privacy.

Article 25 of the European Directive specifies that any transfer of personal data that are being processed or are to be processed after their transfer must attract an adequate level of protection by the jurisdiction to which they are sent. The adequacy of protection is to be evaluated by reference to the nature of the data, the purpose and duration of the proposed processing, the country of origin and of final destination, the general or sectoral regulation in the jurisdiction in question, and the nature and scope of security measures. This immediately endangered the future of business in the largest market on earth, the United States. I return to this difficulty below.

## Sensitive data

Certain items of personal information are intrinsically more sensitive than others, and therefore warrant stronger protection. What might these types of information be? Article 8 of the European Directive requires Member States to prohibit the processing of personal data 'revealing racial or ethnic origin, political opinions, religious or philosophical beliefs, trade union membership, and the processing of data concerning health or sex life'. This restriction is, however, subject to a number of exceptions including, unless domestic legislation explicitly provides otherwise, the provision by the data subject of explicit consent to such processing. It is also permissible when necessary to protect the rights and duties of the controller in the field of employment law, or to protect the 'vital interests' of the data subject.

This is echoed in the legislation of other European jurisdictions. The United Kingdom's Data Protection Act of 1998 classifies as 'sensitive' information relating to the data subject's racial or ethnic origin, political opinions, religious or similar beliefs, membership of a trade union, physical or mental health, sexual life, the commission or alleged commission of any offence, or any proceedings for any offence committed or alleged to have been committed.

Any inventory such as these clearly requires interpretation. Data about the twisted ankle that sent you to the hospital is plainly less sensitive than your HIV-positive status. But a modest degree of common sense ought to ensure that distinctions such as this are drawn.

In view of their high sensitivity, preserving the privacy of medical records is particularly critical. A growing problem concerns the significant number of non-medical personnel who have access to patients' data. They are not always subject to a strict duty of confidence.

Recently the European Court of Human Rights penalized the government of Finland for its failure to protect medical patient data held by a hospital against the risk of unauthorized access. The judgment establishes a connection between the right to privacy under human rights law and the protection of personal information. It held that Article 8 includes a positive duty to ensure the security of personal data. The hospital's filing system contravened Finland's own law that requires hospitals to secure personal data against unauthorized access. The petitioner, a nurse at the hospital where she was being treated for HIV, suspected that her co-workers had discovered that she was HIV-positive by reading her confidential medical records. Although the hospital rules prohibited access to these files, save for purposes of treatment, in practice the records of patients were accessible to all hospital staff.

The Court held that the mere fact that the hospital had an insecure medical records system was sufficient to render it liable for the otherwise unexplained disclosure of the nurse's private medical data.

Equally troubling is the reckless loss of sensitive data stored on disks or memory sticks. In late 2008, for example, disks containing personal information on almost 18,000 National Health Service patients went missing from a North London hospital. The hospital admitted that the disks were lost when they were put in the post!

The records of AIDS patients or those who are HIV-positive are especially sensitive. A number of arguments have, however, been raised to justify the violation of these patients' medical confidentiality. It is urged, in particular, that in order to contain the spread of the disease it may be necessary for doctors to report cases to public health authorities. Indeed, in some jurisdictions, AIDS is a notifiable disease and therefore a legal duty arises to inform authorities of its appearance. The requirement of accurate information is plainly important if research into the causes and proliferation of AIDS is to be effectively conducted. But there is no compelling reason why such data cannot be anonymous. Given the traumatic consequences that their disclosure can produce, the onus should be on the health authority to demonstrate that the benefits outweigh patients' rights to confidentiality.

Indeed, the failure adequately to protect these data may well be counter-productive; many will simply be deterred from being tested for the virus. This will dry up sources of information and, at the same time, contribute indirectly to the further spread of the illness.

Other elementary failures in the security of medical data inspire little confidence in the proper enforcement of the Data Protection Act. A recent survey by two doctors at a top London hospital revealed that three-quarters of them carried unsecured memory sticks with confidential data. Hospital doctors routinely carry memory sticks containing names, diagnoses, X-rays, and treatment details. Of the 105 doctors at their hospital, 92 held memory sticks, with 79 of them containing confidential information. Only 5 of those were protected by passwords.

## Digital data

The ubiquity of computers and computer networks facilitates almost instant storage, retrieval, and transfer of data – a far cry from the world of manual filing systems. More spectacularly, efforts to control the Internet, its operation or content, have been conspicuously unsuccessful. Indeed, its anarchy and resistance to regulation are widely vaunted as its very strength and appeal. Apart from the problem of when it is reasonable to expect that one's conversations are private, the nature of communication on the Internet generates different issues and expectations, and, hence, the need for different solutions.

While the monitoring of digital telephone systems (described in Chapter 1) may appear to be similar to the sending and receiving of email, the use of the Internet poses intractable challenges to regulation. For example, while it is simple to monitor my telephone calls or intercept my letters, the culture of the Internet encourages a range of activities whose observation presents irresistible opportunities for those who wish to supervise or control the private and the sensitive.

## Data protection and privacy

But, you are entitled to ask, what does data protection have to do with privacy? The relationship between the two is not immediately obvious. They plainly overlap; indeed, the latter is routinely invoked as the interest that animates the former. But – even in our information society – it is not always individual privacy that is violated by the collection, use, storage, or transfer of personal data. This is not merely because 'personal data' is widely defined in data-protection statutes to include information about a 'person'

"We have to be forthright with the public. We have to have their confidence. We have to convince them we're working for the common good. *Then* we can invade their privacy."

16. The collection and use of personal data is readily – and often disingenuously – justified as being in the public interest

that is not necessarily 'private'. The simple answer is that in seeking to protect this class of data, information of a genuinely private nature is willy-nilly caught in the net.

Indeed, it is not wholly implausible to suggest that a number of the problems of defining privacy that we have encountered might be more practically resolved under the data protection umbrella.

Think of the cases of *Peck* and Princess Caroline that were discussed in Chapter 4. The European Court of Human Rights considered them under the rubric of Article 8's privacy clause in the European Convention. The central issue was the lawfulness of surreptitious photography in a public place. Data-protection statutes are not fashioned to provide comprehensive protection for individual privacy, but they routinely stipulate that personal data must be collected by means that are both lawful and fair. Such legislation thus affords incidental protection to privacy.

## The American enigma

Despite – or perhaps because of – the magnitude of its information market, the United States has resisted the adoption of data-protection legislation along European lines – at least in the private sector. Its approach of self-regulation is in stark contrast to the comprehensive approach of the European Union model. This is, in part, attributable to a political culture that eschews vigorous regulatory bodies – a situation all too evident in the context of the credit crisis of 2008. It is hard to visualize the approval of the appointment of an independent Federal privacy commissioner.

To avoid a trade war with Europe, the United States created the tranquil-sounding 'Safe Harbor' framework. The scheme was designed to satisfy the EU that US companies endorsing the scheme would offer adequate privacy protection as defined by the European Union data-protection directive (see box). This compromise was approved by the European Union in 2000.

The scheme has attracted a disappointingly small number of American companies, as they dislike the perceived burden it imposes upon them. The EU Commission has observed that a number of US companies fail to abide by the requirement, stating in their publicly available privacy policy that they comply with the seven principles. In addition, these privacy statements do not

# The Safe Harbor principles

1. NOTICE: An organization must inform individuals about the purposes for which it collects information about them, how to contact the organization with any inquiries or complaints, the types of third parties to which it discloses the information, and the choices and means the organization offers to the individuals for limiting its use and disclosure.

2. CHOICE: An organization must offer individuals the opportunity to choose (opt out) whether and how personal information they provide is used or disclosed to third parties (where such use is incompatible with the purpose for which it was originally collected or with any other purpose disclosed to the individual in a notice).

3. ONWARD TRANSFER: An organization may only disclose personal information to third parties consistent with the principles of notice and choice.

4. SECURITY: Organizations creating, maintaining, using or disseminating personal information must take reasonable measures to assure its reliability for its intended use and reasonable precautions to protect it from loss, misuse and unauthorized access, disclosure, alteration and destruction.

5. DATA INTEGRITY: Consistent with these principles, an organization may only process personal information relevant to the purposes for which it has been gathered. To the extent necessary for those purposes, an organization should take reasonable steps to ensure that data is accurate, complete, and current.

6. ACCESS: Individuals must have reasonable access to personal information about them that an organization holds and be able to correct or amend that information where it is inaccurate.

7. ENFORCEMENT: Effective privacy protection must include mechanisms for assuring compliance with the safe harbor principles, recourse for individuals to whom the data relate affected by non-compliance with the principles, and consequences for the organization when the principles are not followed.

generally include all the principles or they translate them incorrectly.

A significant deficiency in the implementation of the 'Safe Harbor' policy is the absence of a complaint enforcement mechanism by those companies that have adopted the system.

## Protecting personal data online

The future is here. The digital world we have created will soon comprise a fibre-optic network that carries – in digital bits – an almost infinite number of television channels, home shopping and banking, interactive entertainment and video games, computer databases, and commercial transactions. This broadband communications network will link households, businesses, and schools to a plethora of information resources. When personal information assumes the form of bits, its vulnerability to misuse, particularly on the Internet, is self-evident.

We have produced a multifunctional telecommunication network that links all existing networks that previously were independent. Moreover, what used to be uni-functional, immobile, and large hardware is now multifunctional, portable, and diminutive: my iPhone allows me to send and receive email, buy and sell, watch television, read newspapers, and so on.

The capacity of computers grows at an astonishing velocity; according to so-called 'Moore's Law', the capacity of a computer is doubled every 18 months, while its price is unaffected. In other words, after a period of 15 years, the processing and storage capabilities of our computers are increased by a factor of 1,000.

## Anonymity and identity

Anonymity is, as was discussed in Chapter 1, an important value. But it is not necessarily absolute anonymity that I seek. Instead, it is what Yves Poullet, Director of the CRID (*Centre de Recherches Informatique et Droit*), calls 'functional non-identifiability' in respect of my message to a certain individual. The notion of anonymity should perhaps therefore be replaced by 'pseudonymity' or 'nonidentifiability'. This right cannot, of course, be absolute. A balance must be struck with the demands of national security, defence, and the detection and prosecution of crime. This is possible by the use of 'pseudo identities' furnished to individuals by specialist service providers who may be required to reveal a user's actual identity when required by the law.

Conventional accounts – understandably – neglect the value and importance of anonymity as a feature of the 'new privacy'. The instability of the subject is a central theme of postmodernism. The Internet appears as a living testament to the ideas of the absence of a universal, unitary truth, and the contingency and diversity of the self that emerge in the writings of postmodernist icons such as Jacques Lacan.

The fluidity of identity on the Internet is among its chief attractions, but there may be increasing pressure to establish who the sender is, especially for commercial purposes. Digital authentication is likely to grow in importance as more business is conducted online.

## The future of data protection

The current data-protection regime sketched above is no panacea. It is ill-equipped to cope with the countless challenges to privacy by the Internet and technological advances in RFID, GPS, mobile telephony, and so on. These developments are admirably described by Poullet, who postulates a new suite of principles to manage these frequently unsettling developments.

The ubiquity and multi-functionality of electronic communication service environments, as well as their interactivity, the international character of networks, services, and equipment producers, and the absence of transparency in terminal and network functioning jeopardize online privacy. Poullet accordingly proposes a number of 21st-century principles that include the principle of encryption and reversible anonymity. This is of critical importance in providing protection against access to the content of our communications. Encryption software has become affordable to the ordinary computer user.

Another principle is that of encouraging technological approaches compatible with or improving the situation of legally protected persons. This could involve requiring that both software and hardware provide the necessary tools to comply with data-protection rules. They ought to include maximum protective features as standard.

This obligation also applies to those who process personal data to select the most appropriate technology for minimizing the threat to privacy. The development of the privacy-enhancing technologies (PETs) described in Chapter 1, ought to be encouraged and subsidized, voluntary certification and accreditation systems established, and ITTs made available at reasonable prices.

Hardware should operate transparently; users should have complete control over data sent and received. They ought, for example, to be able to ascertain easily the extent of chattering on their computers, what files have been received, their purpose, and their senders and recipients. Anyone who has attempted to block pop-up windows will know how frustratingly difficult this process can be. Omitting to activate a cookie suppressor cannot be construed as *carte blanche* consent to their installation.

Our online lives warrant protection equivalent to the consumer laws that we enjoy in the material world. Why should surfers be expected to tolerate profiling, spamming, differential access to services, and so on? Online consumer protection legislation could open the door to a range of services, including the specification of the duties of ISPs, search engines, databases, as well as measures to prevent unfair competition and commercial practices. Moreover, as Poullet argues why should product liability for hardware and software not extend beyond physical and financial harm to incorporate infringements of data-protection norms?

The advent of Web 2.0 has generated a massive explosion in social networking sites such as Facebook and MySpace, video-sharing sites like YouTube and Flickr, for the sharing of photographs and Wikipedia, the online encyclopaedia written by its users. There are plainly privacy costs to be incurred. The members of social networks may be blissfully unaware of the consequences of the widespread dissemination of their personal information. Providers should, of course, inform them how to restrict access to these data. They ought to offer opt-out for general profile data and opt in for sensitive data. Users need to know there is little or no protection against the copying of their personal data, whether or not these data relate to themselves or to others.

Data protection

17. Proposals by the British government to introduce a central database of fingerprints and other personal data have attracted considerable opposition

There are other privacy perils. Facebook, for example, allows users to add gadgets to their profiles and play with third-party applications without leaving the Facebook site. But this gives rise to privacy problems. When a user installs a Facebook application, the application can see anything that the user can see. The application may therefore request information about the user, his or her friends, and fellow network members. There is nothing to stop the owner of the application from collecting, viewing – and misusing – this personal information. The Facebook terms of use agreement urges application developers to refrain from doing this, but Facebook had no way of discovering or preventing them from engaging in these activities. Though under pressure from the Canadian Privacy Commissioner, it has recently amended its privacy policy so that applications cannot access users' friends' profile information without the express permission of each friend. Users generally regard their profiles on social networking sites as a form of self-expression, but they have commercial value to marketing companies, competing networking sites, and identity thieves. Data mining has serious privacy implications: it exposes information that might otherwise be hidden. It is the process of analysing data from different perspectives and summarizing it into information that may be used to increase income, reduce costs, or both. Data-mining software permits users to analyze data from multiple perspectives, categorize it, and evaluate the relationships identified. In other words, it searches for correlations or patterns among numerous fields in large relational databases.

While it is extremely valuable in commercial, medical, or scientific contexts, data mining does create risks to privacy. In the absence of patterns, bits of raw data are largely worthless. But when mining the data reveals a configuration of behaviour that would otherwise be innocuous, the privacy threat is swiftly evident.

# Chapter 6
# The death of privacy?

'Privacy is dead. Get over it.' Thus spake Scott McNealy, CEO of Sun Microsystems. He is not alone; the demise of privacy has been pronounced by an expanding posse of pessimists and soothsayers. A requiem is, however, premature. The invaders are at the gate, but the citadel will not fall without a battle.

## Vital signs

For many privacy advocates, however, privacy still lives and breathes, but requires urgent regeneration. Groups such as Privacy International, the Electronic Frontier Foundation (EFF), the Electronic Privacy Information Center (EPIC), and several others continue to wage a gruelling campaign against the seemingly inexorable conquest of Big Brother. The crusade has become especially challenging since the events of 11 September 2001.

Examples abound. Fears of comprehensive 24-hour monitoring by CCTV were raised in early 2009 by the announcement that to safeguard security at the 2012 Olympic Games in London, the British government has appointed EADS, a defence company, to develop a system, known as DYVINE, that would allow a central police control room to tap in remotely to any CCTV network in London and plot the information on a detailed 3D map. It would include vehicle number-plate recognition cameras as well as private networks, such as those operating in shopping centres and car parks. This will facilitate the tracking of suspects throughout the city. Advanced computer intelligence systems would assist officers by filtering out all but the most relevant CCTV feeds entering the control room, thereby cutting the time normally spent scrambling from one camera to the next.

The anxiety generated by systems such as this focuses on the dangers posed to privacy by the manifold forms of electronic and other forms of monitoring and intrusion discussed in Chapter 1. But there is the equally disconcerting onslaught perpetuated by the media in pursuit of sensationalist gossip discussed in Chapter 4. Both warrant a few brief concluding remarks here.

### Memories are made of bits

Moore's Law and the World Wide Web have changed everything. The world is a very different one from the Cold War world. McLuhan's global village has finally arrived, and our business is everyone's business. Changes in technology allied to changes in ideology and a lack of deference to authority mean that transparency has increased dramatically, and we will not be able to return to opacity in the foreseeable future. If people are aware of the ramifications of what they do, and if they remember that the memory of an action will outlast the moment, and that the audience for a story is much wider than the immediate group of hearers or readers, then they will be able to do what people do so well – negotiate a nuanced set of strategies for disclosing information depending on the context. But they need to be fully aware that the online context is somewhat different from the offline world, in particular with digital 'memories' lasting far out into the future.

K. O'Hara and N. Shadbolt, *The Spy in the Coffee Machine* (Oneworld, 2008), p. 230

# Technology and tranquillity

The pace of technological innovation will continue to increase. This will be accompanied by new and more insidious forms of encroachment on our private lives. But privacy is too fundamental a democratic value for it to be vanquished without a struggle. It is true that, especially in the face of real or perceived threats, many are disposed to trade their privacy for safety or security – even when it is demonstrated, for example, that the proliferation of CCTV cameras has achieved only limited success in curbing crime.

The erosion of privacy therefore tends to occur by quiescent accretion: through apathy, indifference, or tacit support for measures that are packaged as essential or appear innocuous. And we should not pretend that in our digital world the regulation of privacy-invading conduct will be unproblematic; far from it. Online privacy is bound to continue to be vulnerable to a wide range of attacks. Yet cyberspace is prone to some degree of control, not necessarily by law, but through its essential make-up, its 'code': software and hardware that constitutes cyberspace. That code, it is argued by Lessig, can either produce a place where freedom prevails or one of oppressive control. Indeed, commercial considerations increasingly render cyberspace decidedly susceptible for regulation; it has become a location in which conduct is more strongly controlled than in real space. In the end, he maintains, it is a matter for us to determine; the choice is one of architecture: what sort of code should govern cyberspace, and who will control it. And in this respect, the central legal issue is code. We need to choose the values and principles which should animate that code.

Our defences against these depredations will require also the political will to enact – and actively enforce – appropriate legislation and codes of conduct. Existing data-protection laws, where they exist, need constant revision and rejuvenation, and urgent enactment where they do not. The office of privacy or information commissioner requires adequate funding to facilitate the effective oversight of legislative and other threats to privacy, and the proper regulation and provision of advice and information. An appropriately funded, supported, and competent privacy commissioner can play an indispensable role as guardian of our personal data.

The collaboration of software and hardware manufacturers, service providers, and computer users, along with advice and information about how best to safeguard personal information, are critical components of any privacy protection strategy.

The importance of the privacy-enhancing technologies (PETs) to counter privacy-invading technologies (PITs) – described in Chapter 1 – cannot be over-emphasized. Humans create technology. It can therefore both impair and improve our privacy. Firewalls, anti-hacking mechanisms, and other means are the first line of defence. Expressing one's privacy preferences through, for example P3P (see Chapter 1) is another vital tool in safeguarding our vanishing privacy. How does it work? The privacy preference settings panel of 'Privacy Bird', for example, allows you to configure your personal privacy preferences. When it encounters a website that does not match your privacy preferences, a red warning icon appears in your browser title bar. There are three pre-configured settings: low, medium, and high. When you select a setting, a tick or check mark materializes next to the specific items that will trigger warnings under that setting. The low setting generates a warning only at websites that may use health or medical information, or keep marketing or mailing lists from which you cannot be removed. The medium setting includes additional warnings when sites may share your personally identified information, or if a site does not permit you to establish what data they hold about you. The high setting triggers the maximum number of warnings, including at most commercial websites.

Technological methods to facilitate such preferences are emerging, along with instruments by which data collectors are able to acquaint themselves with their responsibilities.

Pressure groups, non-governmental organizations, lobbyists, and privacy advocates of every stripe perform a vital function in raising consciousness of the relentless assaults on privacy.

While the extraordinary capacity of databases and the Web to collect, store, transfer, monitor, link, and match an incalculable amount of our personal information plainly poses considerable risks, technology is simultaneously our adversary and our ally.

## Pursuing paparazzi

The appetite for tittle-tattle is unlikely to decline. It will continue to be fed – both offline and online – by unauthorized disclosures of personal information. The media in their print and digital manifestations, blogs, social networking sites, and other online purveyors of private facts, both voluntary and unsolicited, present intractable challenges to any form of regulation or control.

18. The photographers arrested after pursuing the vehicle in which Princess Diana was killed

The power of the paparazzi shows few signs of diminishing. Though their intrusive conduct is often conflated with the publication of its fruits, there is a widespread recognition that the law is inadequate on both counts.

At least four possible solutions have been advanced. The first seeks to criminalize the activities of invasive journalists and photographers. So, for example, the state of California (whose constitution explicitly protects privacy) enacted an 'anti-paparazzi' law that creates tort liability for 'physical' and 'constructive' invasions of privacy through photographing, videotaping, or recording a person engaging in a 'personal or familial activity'.

A second line of attack attempts to cajole or compel the media to adopt a variety of forms of self-regulation. The protracted efforts, especially in Britain, to achieve this compromise, and so avert legislative controls, have met with little success.

A third approach is legislation along the lines of the American tort of intentional intrusion upon the plaintiff's seclusion or solitude, or into his private affairs. Liability is distinct from that which may attach to the public disclosure, if any, of the information acquired as a result of the intrusion.

A fourth innovative strategy is to hit the paparazzi where it hurts – in their pockets. By denying them copyright in their pictures, the urge both to snoop and publish might be resisted – the images will not be theirs to sell. Thus if a tabloid could re-publish a surreptitiously obtained photograph of a pop star, without having to shell out a fee, the market for such images would plummet significantly. Paparazzi would go to the wall.

There is already a thin, but rather quaint, line of authority in common law jurisdictions that denies copyright to immoral, deceptive, blasphemous, or defamatory material, but it is unlikely to be invoked today. This proposal would enlarge the scope of turpitude that might induce a court to deny protection. But the idea is artificial, unwieldy, and conceptually problematic. If privacy is to be subsumed by copyright, what the law would in most cases be protecting is less the right of privacy than the plaintiff's right of publicity: the right to control the circumstances under which one's image may be bought and sold. The attraction of this propriety approach to the paparazzi problem is understandable; indeed property interests were among the midwives at the birth of the legal idea of privacy. As described in Chapter 3, the first American judgment to recognize that the common law protected privacy involved the tort of appropriation of name or likeness: the use for the defendant's commercial benefit – usually for advertising purposes – of the plaintiff's identity.

But privacy warrants protection in its own right; backdoor remedies will, in the end, be counterproductive. The ideal answer is explicit, carefully drafted legislation that creates civil and criminal sanctions for seriously offensive, intentional, or reckless intrusion into an individual's solitude or seclusion, and the unauthorized publication of personal information. The latter is, of course, always to be balanced against freedom of speech, as discussed in Chapter 4.

Neither at work nor at home are we entitled to assume that our online applications are safe. We must look to both technology and the law to provide shelter. Technology, it has been frequently stated, generates both the malady and part of the cure. And while the law is rarely an adequate tool against the dedicated intruder, the advances in protective software along with the fair information practices adopted by the European Directive, and the laws of several jurisdictions, afford a rational and sound normative framework for the collection, use, and transfer of personal data. It offers a pragmatic analysis of the uses to which personal information is actually put, the manner of its collection, and the legitimate expectations of individuals. These are the questions that will dominate the discussion of privacy long into our uncertain future. How we address them may determine whether or not we live privately ever after.

# Annex

*Affirming* that privacy is a fundamental human right set out in the Universal Declaration of Human Rights, the International Covenant on Civil and Political Rights, and other human rights instruments and national constitutions;

*Reminding* the EU member countries of their obligations to enforce the provisions of the 1995 Data Protection Directive and the 2002 Electronic Communications Directive;

*Reminding* the other OECD member countries of their obligations to uphold the principles set out in the 1980 OECD Privacy Guidelines;

*Reminding* all countries of their obligations to safeguard the civil rights of their citizens and residents under the provisions of their national constitutions and laws, as well as international human rights law;

*Anticipating* the entry into force of provisions strengthening the Constitutional rights to privacy and data protection in the European Union;

*Noting with alarm* the dramatic expansion of secret and unaccountable surveillance, as well as the growing collaboration between governments and vendors of surveillance technology that establish new forms of social control;

*Further noting* that new strategies to pursue copyright and unlawful content investigations pose substantial threats to communications privacy, intellectual freedom, and due process of law;

*Further noting* the growing consolidation of Internet-based services, and the fact that some corporations are acquiring vast amounts of personal data without independent oversight;

*Warning* that privacy law and privacy institutions have failed to take full account of new surveillance practices, including behavioral targeting, databases of DNA and other biometric identifiers, the fusion of data

139

between the public and private sectors, and the particular risks to vulnerable groups, including children, migrants, and minorities;

*Warning* that the failure to safeguard privacy jeopardizes associated freedoms, including freedom of expression, freedom of assembly, freedom of access to information, non-discrimination, and ultimately the stability of constitutional democracies;

Civil Society takes the occasion of the 31st annual meeting of the International Conference of Privacy and Data Protection Commissioners to:

(1) Reaffirm support for a global framework of Fair Information Practices that places obligations on those who collect and process personal information and gives rights to those whose personal information is collected;

(2) Reaffirm support for independent data protection authorities that make determinations, in the context of a legal framework, transparently and without commercial advantage or political influence;

(3) Reaffirm support for genuine Privacy Enhancing Techniques that minimize or eliminate the collection of personally identifiable information and for meaningful Privacy Impact Assessments that require compliance with privacy standards;

(4) Urge countries that have not ratified Council of Europe Convention 108 together with the Protocol of 2001 to do so as expeditiously as possible;

(5) Urge countries that have not yet established a comprehensive framework for privacy protection and an independent data protection authority to do so as expeditiously as possible;

(6) Urge those countries that have established legal frameworks for privacy protection to ensure effective implementation and enforcement, and to cooperate at the international and regional level;

(7) Urge countries to ensure that individuals are promptly notified when their personal information is improperly disclosed or used in a manner inconsistent with its collection;

(8) Recommend comprehensive research into the adequacy of techniques that "deidentify" data to determine whether in practice such methods safeguard privacy and anonymity;

(9) Call for a moratorium on the development or implementation of new systems of mass surveillance, including facial recognition, whole body imaging, biometric identifiers, and embedded RFID tags, subject to a full and transparent evaluation by independent authorities and democratic debate; and

(10) Call for the establishment of a new international framework for privacy protection, with the full participation of civil society, that is based on the rule of law, respect for fundamental human rights, and support for democratic institutions.

# References

## Chapter 1: The assault

'It was reported in early 2009 . . .': *Sunday Times*, 4 January 2009.

'Free conversation is often characterized . . .': L. B. Schwartz, 'On Current Proposals to Legalize Wiretapping' (1954) 103 *University of Pennsylvania Law Review* 157, p. 162.

Examples of characteristics on which biometric technologies can be based: drawn from Roger Clarke, 'Biometrics and Privacy', http://www.anu.edu.au/people/ Roger.Clarke/DV/Biometrics. html

'[A] bit more invasive than a security guard . . .': L. Lessig, *Code and Other Laws of Cyberspace* (New York: Basic Books, 1999), p. 194.

'Imagine if a hacker put together information . . .': E. G. Lush, 'How Cyber-Crime Became a Multi-Billion-Pound Industry', *The Spectator*, 16 June 2007.

Platform for Privacy Preferences (P3P) Project: http://www.w3.org/ P3P/

'It is a complex and confusing protocol . . .', and 'Simple, predictable rules . . .': Electronic Privacy Information Center (EPIC), http:// www.epic.org/reports/prettypoorprivacy.html

## Chapter 2: An enduring value

My attempt to address the intractable problem of defining privacy draws on my serial endeavours to grasp this nettle; some of these works are listed in the section on 'Further reading'.

'The closer people come...': R. Sennett, *The Fall of Public Man* (Harmondsworth: Penguin, 1974), p. 338.

'In ancient feeling...': H. Arendt, *The Human Condition* (Chicago: University of Chicago Press, 1958), p. 38.

'[L]iberalism may be said largely...': S. Lukes, *Individualism* (Oxford: Basil Blackwell, 1973), p. 62.

'One of the central goals...': M. Horwitz, 'The History of the Public/Private Distinction' (1982) 130 *University of Pennsylvania Law Review* 1423, p. 1424.

'[T]he sole end...': J. S. Mill, *On Liberty* (London: Longman, Roberts & Green, 1869), p. 9.

'On any given day...': A. F. Westin, *Privacy and Freedom* (New York: Atheneum, 1967), pp. 34–5.

'[A]n air of injured gentility': H. Kalven, 'Privacy in Tort Law: Were Warren and Brandeis Wrong?' (1966) 31 *Law and Contemporary Problems* 326, p. 329.

The 'claim of individuals, groups...': A. F. Westin, *Privacy and Freedom* (New York: Atheneum, 1967), p. 7.

Privacy consists of 'limited accessibility': R. Gavison, 'Privacy and the Limits of Law' (1980) 89 *Yale Law Journal* 412.

'To the extent that people conceal...': R. Posner, 'The Right of Privacy' (1978) 123 *Georgia Law Review* 393, p. 401.

## Chapter 3: A legal right

*Prince Albert v Strange* (1849) 1H. & W. 1. 64 E.R. 293. On appeal: (1849) 1 Mac. & G. 25, 41 E.R. 1171.

S. D. Warren and L. D. Brandeis, 'The Right to Privacy' (1890) 5 *Harvard Law Review* 196.

'Flour of the family': *Roberson v Rochester Folding Box Co.* 171N.Y. 538; 64N.E. 442 (1902).

Supreme Court of Georgia: *Pavesich v New England Life Insurance Co.*, 122 Ga. 190; 50S.E. 68 (1905).

W. L. Prosser, 'Privacy' (1960) 48 *California Law Review* 383.

Its moral basis as an aspect of human dignity: E. J. Bloustein, 'Privacy as an Aspect of Human Dignity: An Answer to Dean Prosser' (1964) 39 *New York University Law Review* 962.

H. Kalven, 'Privacy in Tort Law: Were Warren and Brandeis Wrong?' (1966) 31 *Law and Contemporary Problems* 326.

*Olmstead v United States* 277 U.S. 438 (1928).

*Katz v United States* 398 U.S. 347 (1967).

*Griswold v Connecticut* 381 U.S. 479 (1965).

*Roe v Wade* 410 U.S. 113 (1973).

'[U]ndoubtedly the best-known case...': R. Dworkin, *Life's Dominion: An Argument about Abortion and Euthanasia* (London: Harper Collins, 1993) pp. 4 and 103.

*Bowers v Hardwick* 478 U.S. 186 (1986).

*Lawrence v Texas* 539 U.S. 558 (2003).

*Report of the Committee on Privacy* (Chairman: K. Younger), Cmnd 5012 (1972) Para. 653.

*Douglas v Hello! Ltd* [2007] 2 W.L.R. 920 (H.L.).

Lord Hoffmann: *Wainwright v Home Office* [2003] U.K.H.L. 53, Para. 34.

The 'final impetus to the recognition of a right of privacy...': *Douglas v Hello! Ltd* [2005] 1 Q.B. 967 at para 111, *per* Sedley LJ.

*Australian Broadcasting Corporation v Lenah Game Meats Pty Ltd* [2001] HCA 63.

*Hosking v Runting and Pacific Magazines NZ Ltd* [2004] CA 101.

*Gaskin v United Kingdom* (1989) 12 E.H.H.R. 36.

*Leander v Sweden* (1987) 9 E.H.H.R. 443.

*Katz v United States* 389 U.S. 347 (1967).

'[T]he party to the conversation...': *Privacy*, Australian Law Reform Commission No. 22, Para. 1128.

*Klass v Federal Republic of Germany* (1978) 2 E.H.H.R 214.

*Malone v United Kingdom* (1984) 7 E.H.R.R. 14.

'[N]ot because we wish to hamper...': S. M. Beck, 'Electronic Surveillance and the Administration of Criminal Justice' (1968) 46 *Canadian Bar Review* 643, p. 687.

## Chapter 4: Privacy and free speech

Some of the discussion on the attempt to reconcile privacy and freedom of expression is based on my *Privacy and Press Freedom* (London: Blackstone, 1995).

*Campbell v Mirror Group Newspapers Ltd* [2004] 2A.C. 457 (H.L.)

*Douglas v Hello! Ltd* [2006] Q.B. 125; [2007] 2 W.L.R. 920 (H.L.).

*Von Hannover v Germany* [2004] E.M.L.R. 379 (E.C.H.R).

*Peck v United Kingdom* [2003] E.M.L.R. 379 (E.C.H.R.).

*Dietemann v Time, Inc.* 449F. 2d 244 (1971).

T. L. Emerson, *The System of Freedom of Expression* (New York: Random House, 1970).

'[A]t most points the law...': T. L. Emerson (above), p. 331.

'Privacy law might be more just...': D. L. Zimmerman, 'Requiem for a Heavyweight: A Farewell to Warren and Brandeis's Privacy Tort' (1983) 68 *Cornell Law Review* 291, pp. 362–4.

'[A]nother approach, and one...': T. L. Emerson, 'The Right of Privacy and Freedom of the Press' (1979) 14 *Harvard Civil Rights-Civil Liberties Law Review* 329, p. 343.

'[S]uffers from a failure...': F. Schauer, *Free Speech: A Philosophical Enquiry* (Cambridge: Cambridge University Press, 1982), p. 56.

'[A] rigorous examination of motives...': E. Barendt, *Freedom of Speech*, 2nd edn. (Oxford: Oxford University Press, 2005), p. 24.

'The principle of the freedom of speech...': A. Meiklejohn, *Political Freedom: The Constitutional Powers of the People* (New York: Oxford University Press, 1965).

'The liberty of the press is indeed essential...': W. Blackstone, 4 *Commentaries on the Laws of England* (1769), pp. 151–2.

*York Times v Sullivan* 376 U.S. 254 at p. 270 per Brennan J (1964).

*Time, Inc. v Hill* 385 U.S. 374 (1967).

'[S]o long as the interest of privacy...': T. Emerson, *Towards a General Theory of the First Amendment* (New York: Vintage, 1966), p. 75.

'It cannot be too strongly emphasised...': *R v Central Independent Television PLC* [1994] Fam. 192 at p. 203 per Hoffmann LJ (as he then was).

'[E]xceptional cases, where the intended...': *Schering Chemicals Ltd v Falkman* [1982] 1 Q.B. 1 at p. 18 per Lord Denning M.R.

'Blackstone was concerned to prevent...': *Schering* (above), p. 39, per Lord Templeman.

'[A]t some point the public interest...': *Sidis v F-R Publishing Co.* 34F. Supp. 19 (S.D.N.Y., 1938); 113F. 2d. 806 at p 809 (1940).

Restatement (Second) of the Law of Torts, §652D (b) and comment h.

*Sipple v Chronicle Publishing Co.* 201 Cal. Rptr 665 (1984).

*Diaz v Oakland Tribune Inc.* 118 Cal. Rptr 762 at p. 773 (1983).

*Ann-Margret v High Society Magazine, Inc.* 498F. Supp. 401 at p. 405 (1980).

'[D]eference to the judgment...': D. L. Zimmerman, 'Requiem for a Heavyweight: A Farewell to Warren and Brandeis's Privacy Tort' (1983) 68 *Cornell Law Review* 291, p. 353.

*Melvin v Reid* 112 Cal. App. 285; 297P. 91 (1931).

*Sidis v F.-R. Publishing Corporation Sidis v F-R Publishing Co.* 34F. Supp. 19 (S.D.N.Y., 1938); 113F. 2d. 806.

*Time, Inc. v Hill* 385 U.S. 374, p. 388 (1967).

## Chapter 5: Data protection

*I v Finland* Eur. Ct. H.R., No. 20511/03 (17 July 2008).
*Eastweek Publisher Ltd v The Privacy Commissioner for Personal Data*
[2000] H.K.C. 692.

## Chapter 6: The death of privacy?

L. Lessig, *Code and Other Laws of Cyberspace* (New York: Basic Books,
1999).
Platform for Privacy Preferences (P3P) Project: http://www.w3.org/
P3P/
Privacy Bird: http://www.privacybird.org

# Further reading

The subject of privacy has attracted the attention of scholars from a wide variety of disciplines, including philosophy, sociology, political science, and law. To avoid swamping the reader with an impossibly vast list of sources, I have restricted this inventory to reasonable – and accessible – proportions, omitting references to the prodigious quantity of periodical literature that grapples with this kaleidoscopic concept (the most essential of which are cited in the 'References' section).

## Chapter 1: The assault

P. Agre and M. Rotenberg (eds.), *Technology and Privacy: The New Landscape* (Cambridge, MA: MIT Press, 1997).

K. Ball and F. Webster (eds.), *The Intensification of Surveillance: Crime, Terrorism and Warfare in the Information Age* (London: Pluto Press, 2003).

C. J. Bennett, *Privacy Advocates: Resisting the Spread of Surveillance* (Cambridge, MA: MIT Press, 2008).

C. J. Bennett and D. Lyon (eds.), *Playing the Identity Card: Surveillance, Security and Identification in Global Perspective* (London: Routledge, 2008).

A. Cavoukian and D. Tapscott, *Who Knows? Safeguarding Your Privacy in a Networked World* (Toronto: Random House, 1995).

S. Davies, *Big Brother: Britain's Web of Surveillance and the New Technological Order* (London: Pan Books, 1996).

W. Diffie and S. Landau, *Privacy on the Line: The Politics of Wiretapping and Encryption* (Cambridge, MA: MIT Press, 2007).

P. Fitzgerald and M. Leopold, *Stranger on the Line: The Secret History of Phone Tapping* (London: The Bodley Head, 1987).

D. Flaherty, *Protecting Privacy in Surveillance Societies: The Federal Republic of Germany, Sweden, France, Canada, and the United States* (Chapel Hill, NC: University of North Carolina Press, 1989).

D. Flaherty, *Protecting Privacy in Two-Way Electronic Services* (London: Mansell Publishing Limited, 1985).

J. Gibb, *Who's Watching You? The Chilling Truth about the State, Surveillance and Personal Freedom* (London: Collins & Brown, 2005).

J. Goldsmith and T. Wu, *Who Controls the Internet? Illusions of a Borderless World* (Oxford: Oxford University Press, 2006).

C. Jennings and L. Fena, *The Hundredth Window: Protecting Your Privacy and Security in the Age of the Internet* (New York: Free Press, 2000).

K. Laidler, *Surveillance Unlimited: How We've Become the Most Watched People on Earth* (Cambridge: Icon Books, 2008).

J. Losek, *The War on Privacy* (Westport, CT: Praeger, 2007).

D. Lyon, *The Electronic Eye: The Rise of Surveillance Society* (Minneapolis, MI: University of Minnesota Press, 1994).

D. Lyon, *Surveillance after September 11* (Cambridge: Polity Press, 2003).

D. Lyon (ed.), *Surveillance as Social Sorting: Privacy, Risk, and Digital Discrimination* (London and New York: Routledge, 2003).

D. Lyon, *Surveillance Society: Monitoring Everyday Life* (Buckingham: Open University Press, 2001).

D. Lyon, *Surveillance Studies: An Overview* (Cambridge: Polity Press, 2007).

D. Lyon, *Theorizing Surveillance: The Panopticon and Beyond* (Uffculme: Willan Publishing, 2006).

R. Mansell and S. Collins (eds.), *Trust and Crime in Information Societies* (Cheltenham: Edward Elgar Publications, 2005).

G. Marx, *Undercover: Police Surveillance in America* (Berkeley, CA, and London: University of California Press, 1992).

M. S. Monmonier, *Spying with Maps: Surveillance Technologies and the Future of Privacy* (Chicago, Ill: University of Chicago Press, 2002).

C. Norris and G. Armstrong, *The Maximum Surveillance Society: The Rise of CCTV* (London: Berg, 1999).

J. Parker, *Total Surveillance: Investigating the Big Brother World of E-spies, Eavesdroppers and CCTV* (London: Piatkus Books, 2000).

Privacy

J. K. Petersen, *Understanding Surveillance Technologies: Spy Devices, Privacy, History and Applications* (Boca Raton, FL: Auerbach, 2007).

J. B. Rule, *Privacy in Peril* (New York: Oxford University Press, 2007).

J. B. Rule, *Private Lives and Public Surveillance* (London: Allen Lane, 1973).

B. Schouten, N. C. Juul, A. Drygajlo, and M. Tistarelli (eds.), *Biometrics and Identity Management* (Heidelberg: Springer, 2008).

D. J. Solove, *The Digital Person: Technology and Privacy in the Information Age* (New York: New York University Press, 2004).

D. J. Solove, M. Rotenberg, and P. Schwartz, *Privacy, Information, and Technology* (New York: Aspen, 2006).

C. J. Sykes, *The End of Privacy* (New York: St Martin's Press, 1999).

D. Thomas and B. B. Loader (eds.), *Cybercrime: Law Enforcement, Security and Surveillance in the Information Age* (London: Routledge, 2000).

R. Whitaker, *The End of Privacy: How Total Surveillance is Becoming a Reality* (New York: New Press, 1999).

## Chapter 2: An enduring value

P. Birks (ed.), *Privacy and Loyalty* (Oxford: Oxford University Press, 1997).

S. Bok, *Secrets: On the Ethics of Concealment and Revelation* (New York: Pantheon, 1982).

A. Etzioni, *The Limits of Privacy* (New York: Basic Books, 1999).

D. Flaherty, *Privacy in Colonial New England* (Charlottesville, VA: University Press of Virginia, 1972).

O. Gandy, Jr, *The Panoptic Sort: A Political Economy of Personal Information* (Boulder, CO: Westview Press, 1993).

J. Griffin, *On Human Rights* (Oxford and New York: Oxford University Press, 2008).

R. F. Hixson, *Privacy in a Public Society: Human Rights in Conflict* (New York: Oxford University Press, 1987).

J. Inness, *Privacy, Intimacy and Isolation* (New York: Oxford University Press, 1992).

L. Lessig, *Code and Other Laws of Cyberspace* (New York: Basic Books, 1999).

L. Lessig, *Code: Version 2.0* (New York: Basic Books, 2006).

A. Moore, *Privacy Rights: Moral and Legal Foundations* (Philadephia, PA: University of Pennsylvania Press, 2009).

B. Moore, *Privacy: Studies in Social and Cultural History* (New York: M. E. Sharp, 1984).

E. Neill, *Rites of Privacy and the Privacy Trade: On the Limits of Protection for the Self* (Montreal and Kingston: McGill-Queen's University Press, 2001).

M. C. Nussbaum, *Hiding from Humanity: Disgust, Shame, and the Law* (Princeton, NJ: Princeton University Press, 2004).

J. Pennock and J. Chapman, *Privacy: Nomos XIII* (New York: Atherton Press, 1971).

J. Rosen, *The Naked Crowd: Reclaiming Security and Freedom in an Anxious Age* (New York: Random House, 2004).

F. Schoeman (ed.), *Philosophical Dimensions of Privacy: An Anthology* (Cambridge: Cambridge University Press, 1984).

F. Schoeman, *Privacy and Social Freedom* (Cambridge: Cambridge University Press, 1992).

R. Sennett, *The Fall of Public Man* (Harmondsworth: Penguin, 1974).

D. J. Siepp, *The Right to Privacy in American History* (Cambridge, MA: Harvard University Press, 1978).

D. J. Solove, *Understanding Privacy* (Cambridge, MA: Harvard University Press, 2008).

R. Wacks, *Law, Morality, and the Private Domain* (Hong Kong: Hong Kong University Press, 2000).

R. Wacks (ed.), *Privacy: The International Library of Essays in Law and Legal Theory*. Volume I: *The Concept of Privacy* (London, Dartmouth, New York: New York University Press, 1993).

A. F. Westin, *Privacy and Freedom* (New York: Atheneum, 1967).

A. F. Westin and M. A. Baker, *Databanks in a Free Society: Computers, Record-Keeping, and Privacy* (New York: Quadrangle, 1972).

J. Young (ed.), *Privacy* (New York: Wiley, 1978).

## Chapter 3: A legal right

A. T. Kenyon and M. Richardson (eds.), *New Dimensions in Privacy Law: International and Comparative Perspectives* (Cambridge: Cambridge University Press, 2006).

J. L. Mills, *Privacy: The Lost Right* (New York: Oxford University Press, 2008).

P. Regan, *Legislating Privacy: Technology, Social Values and Public Policy* (Chapel Hill, NC: University of North Carolina Press, 1995).

J. B. Rule and G. Greenleaf (eds.), *Global Privacy Protection: The First Generation* (London: Edward Elgar, 2008).

R. Wacks, *Personal Information: Privacy and the Law* (Oxford: Clarendon Press, 1989).

R. Wacks (ed.), *Privacy: The International Library of Essays in Law and Legal Theory.* Volume II: *Privacy and the Law* (London, Dartmouth, New York: New York University Press, 1993).

R. Wacks, *The Protection of Privacy* (London: Sweet & Maxwell, 1980).

## Chapter 4: Privacy and free speech

L. Alexander, *Is There a Right of Freedom of Expression?* (Cambridge: Cambridge University Press, 2005).

E. Barendt, *Freedom of Speech*, 2nd edn. (Oxford: Oxford University Press, 2007).

C. Calvert, *Voyeur Nation: Media, Privacy, and Peering in Modern Culture* (New York: Basic Books, 2004).

H. Jenkins, *Convergence Culture: Where Old and New Media Collide* (New York: New York University Press, 2008).

J. Rozenberg, *Privacy and the Press* (Oxford: Oxford University Press, 2005).

D. J. Solove, *The Future of Reputation: Gossip, Rumor, and Privacy on the Internet* (New Haven, CT: Yale University Press, 2007).

H. Tomlinson, *Privacy and the Media. The Developing Law* (London: Matrix Chambers, 2002).

R. Wacks, *Privacy and Press Freedom* (London: Blackstone Press, 1995).

## Chapter 5: Data protection

C. Bennett, *Regulating Privacy. Data Protection and Public Policy in Europe and the United States* (Ithaca, NY: Cornell University Press, 1992).

C. Bennett and C. Raab, *The Governance of Privacy: Policy Instruments in Global Perspective*, 2nd edn. (Cambridge, MA: MIT Press, 2006).

M. Berthold and R. Wacks, *Hong Kong Data Privacy Law: Territorial Regulation in a Borderless World*, 2nd edn (Hong Kong: Sweet & Maxwell Asia, 2003).

L. Bygrave, *Data Protection Law: Approaching its Rationale, Logic and Limits* (The Hague: Kluwer Law International, 2002).

P. Schwartz and J. Reidenberg, *Data Protection Law: A Study of United States Data Protection* (Dayton: Michie, 1996).

## Chapter 6: The death of privacy?

S. Garfinkel, *Database Nation: The Death of Privacy in the Twenty-First Century* (Sebastopol, CA: O'Reilly, 2000).

S. Gutwirth, *Privacy and the Information Age* (Lanham, MD: Rowman & Littlefield, 2002).

B. Kahin and C. Nesson (eds.), *Borders in Cyberspace: Information Policy and the Global Information Infrastructure* (Cambridge, MA: MIT Press, 1997).

G. Laurie, *Genetic Privacy: A Challenge to Medico-Legal Norms* (Cambridge: Cambridge University Press, 2002).

D. Lyon, C. Bennett, and R. Grant (eds.), *Visions of Privacy: Policy Choices for the Digital Age* (Toronto: University of Toronto Press, 1998).

K. O'Hara and N. Shadbolt, *The Spy in the Coffee Machine: The End of Privacy as We Know It* (Oxford: Oneworld, 2008).

J. Rosen, *The Unwanted Gaze: The Destruction of Privacy in America* (New York: Random House, 2000).

C. J. Sykes, *The End of Privacy* (London: St Martin's Press, 2000).

J. Zittrain, *The Future of the Internet: And How to Stop It* (London: Allen Lane, 2008).

## Websites

Electronic Privacy Information Center (EPIC) http://www.epic.org

Privacy International http://www.privacyinternational.org

Privacy Rights Clearinghouse http://www.privacyrights.org

American Civil Liberties Union http://www.aclu.org/privacy

Roger Clarke's Dataveillance and Information Privacy Pages http://www.anu.edu.au/people/Roger.Clarke/DV

Electronic Frontier Foundation (EFF) http://www.eff.org

Health Privacy Project (HPP) http://www.healthprivacy.org

Anti-Phishing Working Group http://www.antiphishing.org

The Privacy Forum privacy@vortex.com

Institute for the Study of Privacy Issues (ISPI) http://www.PrivacyNews.com

Medical Privacy Coalition http://www.medicalprivacycoalition.org

People for Internet Responsibility (PFIR) http://www.pfir.org

Privacy News and Information http://www.privacy.org

World Privacy Forum http://www.worldprivacyforum.org

Further reading

# Index